REMEMBER WHO YOU ARE

ARRON CHAMBERS
REMEMBER WHO YOU ARE

unleashing the power of an identity-driven life

Standard® PUBLISHING
Bringing The Word to Life

Cincinnati, Ohio

Published by Standard Publishing, Cincinnati, Ohio
www.standardpub.com

Printed in the United States of America
Project editor: Lynn Lusby Pratt
Cover and interior design: The Design Works Group

ISBN 978-0-7847-2065-3

Library of Congress Cataloging-in-Publication Data

Chambers, Arron.
Remember who you are : unleashing the power of an identity-driven life / Arron Chambers.

    p. cm.

ISBN 978-0-7847-2065-3 (perfect bound)
1. Identification (Religion) 2. Christian life. I. Title.
BV4509.5.C43 2007

   248.4—dc22   2007006238

13 12 11 10 09 08 07   9 8 7 6 5 4 3 2 1

To the late Dr. Roger Chambers—

my mentor, my example, my hero, my friend, and my dad.

Thank you for remembering who you were. I'll never forget you.

I love you, Dad.

And to my children: Ashton, Levi, Sylas, and Payton —

I am excited about who you are and who you're becoming.

I can't wait to ooh and aah as you soar.

I love you.

ACKNOWLEDGMENTS

Perhaps you've heard the story about the proud woodpecker who was tapping away at a dead tree when a storm moved in, the sky turned black, and the thunder began to roll. Undaunted, the woodpecker kept right on working. Suddenly a bolt of lightning struck the old tree, splintering it into hundreds of pieces. Startled but unhurt, the haughty bird flew off, screeching to his feathered friends, "Hey, everyone, look what I did! Look what I did!"

I'd live each day with the fear of being struck by lightning if I ever said anything to suggest that I could have written and delivered this book all by myself. This book is the result of the influence, encouragement, support, love, investment, generosity, flexibility, and talent of a myriad of beautiful people.

Rhonda, my wife, I cherish and adore you. My life would be a joke without you. You are an extraordinary woman who makes life in our home but an earlier Heaven. No one knows the sacrifices you make each time I embark on a project like this—but I do, and I'm so very grateful. I love you, babe.

Ashton, Levi, Sylas, and Payton, I wouldn't trade you for all the money in the world. Have fun storming the castle!

Linda Chambers, my mom, you are the strongest and most Christlike woman I know. I am who I am because you are who you are. I love you.

John and Mary Smith, my in-laws, you are amazing. I'm so grateful for the way you love my family. I'm holding you to your promise about the lava lamp!

My siblings, their spouses, and children are thoroughbreds all. Leigh-Angela, Jeff, and Hunter Holbrook; Leslie, Shan, Taylor, Connor, and Kendall Wood; Adam, Patricia, and Elias Chambers—It's impossible for you to know how much I love you.

My brothers-in-law, sisters-in-law, and children—Mark, Lori, Jessi, Jedidiah, Josiah, Sophi; David, Jan, Ethan, Savanna; Phillip, Tonia, Madyson, Morgan, Makenna—Thanks for helping to care for my kids while I wrote.

Tamela Hancock Murray, a great author and agent, thank you for believing in me since day one and for all you did to make this book a reality.

Twila Sias, my "reader," I cherish our almost-thirty-year friendship more and more each day. You are a beautiful person. I love you, friend.

Joe and Sue Sutherland, my mentors, thanks for your honesty, your example, your encouragement, your guidance, and your friendship.

Dale Reeves, Lynn Pratt, Mark Taylor, Paul Williams, and the rest of the team at Standard Publishing—I knew I'd love working with you, but I didn't realize it would be this much fun. You do excellent work.

Doctors Ben and Sherri Lerner, thanks for all the amazing things you've allowed God to do through you for me and my family.

Mark Atteberry, you are a wonderful author and a more wonderful friend.

The staff and leadership of Southside Christian Church—Eli Reyes, Melissa Clark, Susie Richetti, Joshua J. Van Tassel, Elliott Blount, Terry Allcorn, Travis Jacob, Marvin Lawton, Steve Long, and Randy Patterson—I loved serving with you.

To my church family at Christ's Church, I'm happy to be on your team. It's going to be a wonderful adventure.

Thanks, Linda Stark and the library staff of Florida Christian College; President Wetzel and the library staff at Emmanuel School of Religion; Andrew and Jamie Peterson, for the oceans of love and all of those late-night discussions through which we fixed the world; Terry and Tammy Davis, for sudoku, *A Mighty Wind,* Ci Ci's Pizza, and your love; Books-A-Million in Johnson City, Tennessee, for not throwing me out. (Glenn, I'm still not convinced you're not an angel.)

Thank you for reading this book. If I had to pick from all the readers in the world, I'd pick you every time. Be blessed.

Without each contribution, this book would not exist—and I wouldn't be able to proclaim to the world, "Hey, everyone, look what we did!"

For most who live, hell is never knowing who they are.

—CALVIN MILLER, *The Singer*

CONTENTS

BEFORE WE START

REMINDER TO REMEMBER

Amnesia is a rare, medical condition in which a person can't remember anything. People with amnesia can't remember where they live, how old they are, or even *who* they are. Amnesia is a tragic disorder because without an identity the victim of amnesia has nothing. No home, no birthday, no job, no past, no future, no purpose . . .

OK, I know what you might be thinking—the prospect of having your past wiped away seems a little bit liberating. Maybe you don't like who you've become, and you think life could be much easier if you could wipe the slate clean. You'd love to walk away from your problems and start over. You'd love to just forget who you are. No identity, no messed up marriage. No identity, no rebellious children to break your heart. No identity, no debt. No identity, no taxes. No identity, no in-laws. No identity, no personal history full of poor choices and poor judgment.

But also . . . no identity, no purpose.

Amnesia is not a blessing; it's a curse.

When people don't know who they are, they don't know why they're here. Identity gives life purpose.

I read in the Honolulu *Star-Bulletin* about a man cursed with amnesia.[1] He thinks his name is William. He was found facedown on the beach, with a head injury and no identification. He doesn't know how old he is, where he's from, or how he came to be in Hawaii. He has only sketchy memories of anything prior to 1980. Police have tried matching William's fingerprints to missing people, and hospital officials have chased every name, phone number, and address he can remember. All dead ends. The article says that although he's not sure of his name, he has tested at a genius-level IQ. The article includes his picture. It shows a dark-haired, nice-looking man with a blank stare. His expression seems . . . lifeless, hopeless, and sad. He looks like a man who doesn't know who he is.

He doesn't.

Do *you*?

Do you know who you are? Or have you lost yourself in the process of trying to live?

My parents made me who I am today. They gave me moral direction, confidence, a strong spiritual foundation, and a clear sense of who I am. My dad had a phrase that he said all the time. He especially loved to say it as I headed out the door on a hot date with my girlfriend. He'd say, "Son, remember who you are." Even though he's been gone for almost twenty years, I can still see his face and hear those words as if they were spoken this morning.

"Remember who you are."

Those words were meant to protect me. Those words were a not-so-subtle reminder to be careful. Those words were an anchor for my soul.

Who was I? I was a Christian. I was a member of a church. I was a member of a family. I was the son of Roger, who was a preacher and a well-respected Bible college professor. I was the son of Linda, a church secretary. I was the grandson of godly grandparents. I was the grandson of a preacher. I was the great-grandson of a preacher. I was the great-great-grandson of a preacher.

When my dad said, "Remember who you are," I knew that he was really saying, "May your strong sense of identity keep you from making poor choices that will rob you of the glorious purpose God has for your life."

My identity gave my life purpose.

As I remembered who I was, I made good choices . . . most of the time. I didn't know exactly what I wanted to do with my life, but I knew that God had a plan. I knew that one bad choice could be disastrous. I knew that I was special to God. I knew that if I'd only seek his will and try to follow him, I'd eventually find myself fulfilling his purpose for my life.

Who am I today? I am a Christian. I am a husband. I am a father. I am a son. I am

My identity gave my life purpose.

a grandson. I am a preaching minister. I am a writer. My identity gives my life purpose. When I get up each day, although I may not know what to wear, where my other sock is, why my twelve-year-old daughter is so emotional, where to find my keys, or how to operate the microwave, I *know* why I'm on this planet.

Do you remember who you are?

God wants you to.

Throughout the Bible, God tries to give us a clear sense of identity by reminding us of who we are. He reminds us that we are made "in his own image" (Genesis 1:27). He reminds us that we are his sheep and he is our shepherd who prepares "a table before [us] in the presence of [our] enemies" (Psalm 23:5). He reminds us that we are so special, "he gave his one and only Son, that whoever believes in him shall not perish but have eternal life" (John 3:16).

He has to remind us because we forget so easily.

We get busy, and we forget who we really are.

We get hurt, and we forget who we really are.

We find ourselves in the midst of trials, and we lose ourselves—forgetting who we are.

But our identity in Christ is power.

Too many teens have been convinced that they are simply products of chance, animals who have survived only by being smarter and bigger than millions of other insignificant creatures who came from a slimy creature who found a way to crawl out of a muddy puddle millions of years ago. This book aims to convince us that we are divine reflections of God—created *on* purpose *with* purpose.

Too many adults have been convinced that they exist only to eat, sleep, work, and barbecue by the pool on Labor Day. Somehow and somewhere, while they weren't paying attention, life morphed from a magical world in which they played, hoped, and imagined their way through each day into a dreary world full of appointments, bills, anti-depressants, and loved ones who no longer come home for Christmas. This book is a reminder that we were created to live dynamic lives full of dreams, purpose, laughter, and hope.

Too many Christians seem to have been convinced that the purpose of the Christian's life is to not make God angry. To these fearful faithful, God has become a mean man with big, flat-soled shoes. And we are roaches—wretches—scurrying around his house, hoping we don't do anything that will cause him to squash us. In this book we'll recall who God really is and who we really are. We were not created to be destroyed but to be enjoyed. We are not accidents; we are on purpose. We are not ordinary; we are extraordinary. We are not worthless; we are priceless. We must remember who we are!

Oh, by the way . . . William, the man who was found facedown on a beach in Honolulu, apparently started remembering who he was a few months after they found him. His real name is Philip.[2]

If William—I mean, Philip— can start remembering, there's hope for you too.

WHAT ON EARTH AM I WRITING THIS FOR?

I've read—and enjoyed—Rick Warren's book *The Purpose Driven Life: What on Earth Am I Here For?* Our church is one of the more than thirty thousand congregations that have participated in the 40 Days of Purpose program. It was a positive and unifying experience that more than doubled the number of our small groups and the number of people involved in small groups.

The Purpose Driven Life has not sold more than twenty-four million copies, been translated into more than fifty-six languages, and been one of the world's best-selling books for multiple years by accident. People are looking for purpose. They want a reason to get out of bed. They want a reason to go to work. They want a reason to come home. They want their lives to have a *what* People wondered, *What on earth am I here for?* and God answered through a humble minister from California and a simple book on purpose.

As much as I enjoyed reading the book and participating in the program, there was something that felt premature about *The Purpose Driven Life* . . . like the cart was where the horse should have been.

While reading *The Purpose Driven Life,* I couldn't stop thinking, *This is great stuff for people who want to know what they're here for, but what about the people who want to know who they are?* Life needs purpose. We need purpose. But before we need purpose, we need identity. That's who my heart beats for—the person who needs an identity. Identity is a powerful and creative force.

Identity precedes maturity.

Identity precedes hope.

Identity precedes peace.

Identity precedes purpose.

I believe that it's not until people realize *who* they are that they will begin to wonder *why* they are. I have a burden for the countless people who look in the mirror and don't see an extraordinary person looking back.

So . . . I started to write this book to encourage those who are yet to see value in a *purpose-driven* life because they are yet to see the value of *their* lives. I wrote this book for those who aren't sure they really matter. Before we can do anything that really matters, we need to know that *we* really matter. We must *be* someone who really matters or our actions won't really matter.

And the truth is, we all matter!

So what's the matter? Well, the matter—I mean, the problem—is that we sometimes struggle with something that religious people have struggled with since belief systems began. Sometimes we are good at *doing,* but bad at *being.*

This was the Pharisees' problem. Concerning them, Jesus said in Matthew 23:

- "Woe to you, teachers of the law and Pharisees, you hypocrites! You travel over land and sea to win a single convert, and when he becomes one, you make him twice as much a son of hell as you are" (v. 15).

- "Woe to you, teachers of the law and Pharisees, you hypocrites! You give a tenth of your spices—mint, dill and cummin. But you have neglected the more important matters of the law—justice, mercy and faithfulness. You should have practiced the latter, without neglecting the former" (v. 23).

- "Woe to you, teachers of the law and Pharisees, you hypocrites! You clean the outside of the cup and dish, but inside they are full of greed and self-indulgence" (v. 25).

- "Woe to you, teachers of the law and Pharisees, you hypocrites! You are like whitewashed tombs, which look beautiful on the outside but on the inside are full of dead men's bones. . . . In the same way, on the outside you appear to people as righteous but on the inside you are full of hypocrisy and wickedness" (vv. 27, 28).

The Pharisees knew what on earth they were here for.

They were evangelizing: *You travel over land and sea to win a single convert . . .*

They were giving: *You give a tenth of your spices . . .*

They thought they were living pure lives: *You clean the outside of the cup and dish . . .*

They were public examples of righteousness: *(You) look beautiful on the outside . . .*

They knew their purpose, but they had forgotten who they were!

Jesus' condemnation is not based entirely on what they were doing (or not doing), but on who they were being (or not being). Jesus begins six of the seven woes in Matthew 23 by saying, "Woe to you, teachers of the law and Pharisees, you hypocrites!"

Hypocrites.

Ouch!

And Jesus would know. He sees the heart, so hypocrisy can't be hidden from him beneath fancy clothes, religious

Purpose without identity can lead to a hypocritical existence.

words, and righteous acts. He knows who we really are.

I wish we all did.

Purpose without identity can lead to a hypocritical existence. The Pharisees knew what on earth they were here for—teaching the law to God's people, observing the Sabbath, praying, and tithing—but they had forgotten who on earth they were. They had works but no faith, and works without faith are just as dead as faith without works is.

What if they had really known who they were? What if they had looked at their reflections in the well and seen men of God? What if—based on that identity—they had lived as men of God?

Their lives would have been respected.

Their prayers would have resonated.

Their tithes would have been blessed.

And the Pharisees would be remembered favorably both for who they were and for what they did.

Purpose without identity leads to actions without context, at best, and pharisaical behavior at worst. Because I want to live a purpose-driven life, I seek first to live an identity-driven life. The goal is real purpose, driven by clear identity every day of every year of every life, which—according to the latest studies—will last about 28,470 days.

You can remember who you are if you remember what you've read in this book. And the best way for you to remember what you've read is to interact with it and act on what you've read. So this book is designed to be experienced, not just read.

Each chapter ends with two pages titled "Questions About Who You Are." The pages have been prepared to suit either personal study and reflection or group study and discussion. The questions are designed to be answered immediately after reading the corresponding chapter and will provide an opportunity to experience what you've just read. I encourage you to integrate the creative ideas that are suggested.

Wanna unleash the power of an identity-driven life?

Keep reading.

YOU ARE HUMAN
The difference between Cooper and me

> God said, "Let us make man in our image,
> in our likeness, and let them rule over the
> fish of the sea and the birds of the air, over the
> livestock, over all the earth, and over all the
> creatures that move along the ground."
>
> GENESIS 1:26

A mother bird feeds her young by regurgitating food into their mouths.

A pig sleeps in its own waste.

A cat bathes itself with its tongue.

A male lion will eat all of his male sons to ensure that there are no threats to his leadership of the pride.

In my house we have to make sure that the lid of the toilet is always down because our cat likes to drink out of the toilet.

And in my house we know where all the single socks have gone: our dog eats them! No lie. I have the proof, or at least I can show you the proof the next time I take Cooper out for a walk. It's bizarre.

Animals do the strangest things. Do you know how dogs greet each other? What are they thinking? Well, I've done some research . . .

If you could read a cow's mind, I know you'd hear her thinking, *My life stinks. I know this is not going to end well. I like grass. Why is that bird following me around? I don't know how I can be so fat when all I'm eating is this stupid grass!*

If you could read a male French poodle's mind, you'd hear him lamenting, *I look like such a sissy!*

If you could read a bird's mind, you'd hear, *I just have to hold it until I find Arron's car.*

If you could read my cat's mind, here's what you'd hear: *I'm the ruler of the world! Bow down! Worship me!*

I read that fish have no short-term memory, so here's what my fish is thinking: *Cool. Look at the new diver. He has bubbles coming out of his head.*

He circles the tank.

Cool. Look at the new diver. He has bubbles coming out of his head.

He circles the tank.

Cool. Look at the new diver. He has bubbles coming out of his head.

Yes, animals think and do some stupid things, but I'm really not too concerned about what animals are thinking. I *am* concerned about what you're thinking.

Too many people act like animals because they've believed a lie.

THINKING TOO LITTLE OF OURSELVES

Charles Darwin said, "We must, however, acknowledge, as it seems to me, that man with all his noble qualities . . . still bears in his bodily frame the indelible stamp of his lowly origin."[1] I reject the theory of evolution in favor of creation by intelligent design.

Unlike the account of creation, the theory of evolution is ever-changing. Here's the latest version:

Six hundred million years ago an explosion sent debris rocketing through space.

That debris became planets, suns, and moons.

On earth a primordial soup formed, which contained all the chemicals necessary to form a basic kind of life.

After much time, that material slammed together in just the right way and with

> **Whenever I hear evolutionists say "millions and millions of years," I can't help but think that what they are really saying is "bibbidi-bobbidi-boo!"**

just the right kind of energy, and life developed on this planet.

A one-celled organism evolved to a more complex organism and kept evolving from species to species, always growing more complex and able.

Some of these organisms died out, and some survived.

Sixty-five million years ago dinosaurs died out.

Millions and millions of years passed . . .

Whenever I hear evolutionists say "millions and millions of years," I can't help but think that what they are really saying is "bibbidi-bobbidi-boo!" They really can't explain how a one-celled organism evolved into an organism that can learn how to ride a bike, work geometry, figure out the United States tax code, solve a Rubik's cube, fall in love, and feel guilty in the fourth grade for stealing a pack of gum from the 7-Eleven on Corrine Drive on a Tuesday afternoon. They can't explain it because they don't have the transitional forms and other key evidence to support the theory. Instead, they just insert the magic words *millions and millions of years* and hope that we'll believe it is possible—given enough time—for an ethics professor at Harvard to evolve from primordial soup.

If logic tells us that it's impossible for a gecko to become an eagle in one year or one thousand years or one hundred thousand years, why are some people so willing to believe that a lizard could sprout wings and fly, given millions and millions of years? Because we're intimidated by time and the prospect of having to defend what we have not seen. None of us were there, so no human being is in a position to speak authoritatively on the subject.

All laws of science begin with observation. So since no human being was around to observe the origin of an eagle, a lizard, or a human, we have to settle for the fact that all theories of origins are statements of faith. We just have to decide for ourselves which theory makes the most sense, based on what we have seen and experienced:

"In the beginning God created the heavens and the earth."

or

"Bibbidi-bobbidi-boo!"

But I digress. On with the rest of the latest version of the evolution theory. (Drum roll, please.) Two million years ago homo sapiens evolved from an apelike creature who existed five to eight million years ago.

Does this make you feel better, or worse, about yourself?

A group of young boys built a tree house as the headquarters for a new club and began the all-important task of making a list of the club rules. Their list of only two rules reflected a lot of wisdom. Rule 1 was not a surprise, considering the fact that these were, in fact, young boys; and there's nothing more disgusting to young boys than young, cootie-carrying girls. But rule 2 was surprisingly profound.

H Street Clubhouse Rules

1. No girls allowed.

2. Nobody act too big or too small. Everybody just act medium.

Can you imagine what this world would be like if everybody "acted medium"? There would be no upper class. No lower class. No first-class seating on an airplane. No reserved parking spaces. No titles. No end-zone celebrations. No limousines. No roped-off areas in the stadium and no gated communities.

Jesus acted medium. And one night that attitude resulted in his being surrounded by clean feet and humbled friends. John 13:1-5 says,

> It was just before the Passover Feast. Jesus knew that the time had come for him to leave this world and go to the Father. Having loved his own who were in the world, he now showed them the full extent of his love.
>
> The evening meal was being served, and the devil had already prompted Judas Iscariot, son of Simon, to betray Jesus. Jesus knew that the Father had put all things under his power, and that he had come from God and was returning to God; so he got up from the meal, took off his outer clothing, and wrapped a towel around his waist. After that, he poured water into a basin and began to wash his disciples' feet, drying them with the towel that was wrapped around him.

Jesus knew who he was, where he came from, and where he was going, so he picked up a basin, a towel . . . and eventually a cross. Jesus was "acting medium." He wasn't thinking too highly of himself, but he also wasn't thinking too lowly of himself. He knew what we often forget: "that he had come from God

> **Jesus knew who he was, where he came from, and where he was going.**

and was returning to God" (John 13:3).

Yes, too many of us think too highly of ourselves, but too many of us think too lowly of ourselves as well. We forget that we have come from God too. Not from his person—like Christ did—but from his creative mind. He purposed us. He imagined us. He dreamed of us, and he created us with words, clay, love, and intrinsic value.

We are not God, but we are not animals either.

In brokenness I've proclaimed, "Lord, I'm just a worm. I'm nothing." But my proclamation is not true. I am neither a worm nor nothing. I am something. We are something. We are special. We are human.

We learn from the account of Adam and Eve that Satan wants to destroy us by convincing us that we can be like God. But he also wants to destroy us by trying to convince us of just the opposite: that we are *unlike* God.

> When Satan gets us to think too lowly of ourselves—believing that we are only evolved animals— the results are horrific.

When Satan gets us to think too lowly of ourselves—believing that we are only evolved animals— the results are horrific.

When humans behave like animals . . . we have sex whenever the urge overtakes us.

We act without thinking.

We follow the pack.

We give in to every impulse.

We explode with rage.

We act only in our best interest.

We kill the unwanted, the weak, the sick, and anyone who is viewed as a threat.

We have no purpose but survival, no desire but pleasure.

We expect nothing from ourselves but animalistic behavior, so we throw condoms at teens, legalize prostitution, legalize harmful drugs, redefine marriage, legislate immorality, remove the Ten Commandments, and accept that looting after a hurricane is an appropriate response to a natural disaster.

Satan is a liar. One of his goals has been to convince you that there is no real difference between you and the millions of animal species on this planet. He has convinced many that the only reason we own so much, live on the best land, wear clothes, drive imports, walk upright, and develop places like Walt Disney World is because we're the fittest, strongest, and best organized group of animals on this planet.

We are not God, and we must never allow ourselves to think otherwise. As the apostle Paul points out, we must maintain a proper understanding of who we are and who we are not: "Your attitude should be the same as that of Christ Jesus: Who, being in very nature God, did not consider equality with God something to be grasped, but made himself nothing, taking the very nature of a servant, being made in human likeness. And being found in appearance as a man, he humbled himself and became obedient to death—even death on a cross!" (Philippians 2.5-8).

We can never be like God, but we can never be completely unlike him either. After all, we were made in his image.

IMAGE OF GOD

"God created man in his own image, in the image of God he created him; male and female he created them" (Genesis 1:27).

I've always wanted to be like my dad.

When I was a child, one of my dad's friends would occasionally stop me, smile, pat me on the hand, and sweetly say, "You remind me so much of your father." I felt big and small at the same time.

My mom's photo album contains several pictures of me wearing my dad's shoes on my tiny feet. I wanted to be just like him, so I put on his clothes, tried to walk in his footsteps as we walked down the street, and shaved with him long before I needed to.

I'm no longer a child, but I still want to be like my dad—even though he died almost twenty years ago. He was good. He was funny. He was kind. He was honest. He was smart. He was wise. He was godly.

Do you want to be like your Father? I'm not talking about your father; I'm talking about your *Father.*

Some earthly fathers are not worthy of imitation. They are not good, funny, kind, honest, smart, wise, or godly. Too many children spend too much time in a desperate attempt to shed any resemblance their lives have to the men who fathered them. They hope that in distorting their images, they will eliminate any chance of ever being compared to their fathers.

Sons of a macho father may act effeminate.

Daughters of a weak father may act masculine.

Sons of a mean father may become comedians.

Daughters of an authoritarian father may rebel.

My heavenly Father is amazing. I love everything about him. His voice strengthens me. His words comfort me. His blessings astound me. His image on my life is something I cherish. I long to be like him more and more each day. I long for someone, someday, to say, "You remind me so much of your Father."

BLESSED BY GOD

Genesis 1:28 says that God blessed Adam and Eve. We obviously don't truly understand what the word *bless* means, because we say it after someone sneezes. I think that blessing someone after he sneezes is like playing marbles with diamonds. The word *bless* is much too extraordinary to use it chiefly as a superstitious reaction to an ordinary—and oft recurring—sternutation typically caused by an irritation in the throat, lungs, or in the passages of the nose. Can I get an "Amen!"

The word *bless* comes from the Hebrew word *barak,* which means "to kneel"—because the one who was being blessed would kneel before the one blessing. To bless someone is to wish upon him special favor.

When you were created, the most powerful and most loving being in the universe looked down as you kneeled before him, and said, "Bless you." That's nothing to sneeze at!

> **Nothing is more essential to a child's identity than a father's blessing.**

Do we really understand what this means? It changes everything.

If you're a daughter who never received the "blessing" from your father, you know the feminine insecurity that results from not knowing for sure if your father really loves you.

If you're a son who never received the "blessing" from your father, you know the doubts that stalk your manhood.

Nothing is more essential to a child's identity than a father's blessing, because a father's blessing confirms that he or she is accepted, approved of, and loved.

When God "blessed" you at your creation, he testified for all time that you have his acceptance, approval, and love. God wishes upon you special favor. God wants the best for you. He wants all of your dreams to come true.

ENTRUSTED BY GOD

I'm jealous of my friend Steve Long. Steve's dog obeys him. Gator is a 150-pound bull mastiff who doesn't do anything without Steve's permission. One night when I was at Steve's house, Gator started to walk into the room in which we were meeting. Steve said, "Gator, out!" Gator stopped, turned around, and left the room.

Mystified, I asked, "How did you do that?"

You have to understand that I have a 20-pound dachshund who has perfected the art of ignoring me. I say, "Sit," and he stands on his hind legs, leans against the wall, pulls out a cigarette, lights it, blows smoke in my face, crosses his front paws, and says, "Make me."

So when Steve replied without any hesitation or doubt, "I'm the boss," I was stunned. Could it really be that easy?

Well . . . "God said, 'Let us make man in our image, in our likeness, and *let them rule over* the fish of the sea and the birds of the air, over the livestock, over all the earth, and over all the creatures that move along the ground.' . . . God blessed them and said to them, 'Be fruitful and increase in number; fill the earth and subdue it. *Rule over* the fish of the sea and the birds of the air and over every living creature that moves on the ground'" (Genesis 1:26, 28, emphasis added).

> You and I are carriers of the life breath of God.

In Steve's three little words and this Scripture, I found the secret to successful pet care. My philosophy changed. My relationship with Cooper had been unpleasant because I was working *my* plan and not God's. It was my plan for me to be Cooper's friend, but it was God's plan for me to be Cooper's boss. Cooper is not a person; he's a dog.

I know that's simple, but it's also profound. Cooper and I are very different in nature and in value. You and I are special and more valuable than animals. God entrusted us with the job of ruling over the animals on this planet because we are *not* animals.

The difference between Cooper and me is one of the most powerful proofs of the presence of God. The difference between Cooper and me—and between animals and humans in general—is what C. S. Lewis called "oughtness," or having a sense of moral obligation. Humans are fit to rule because humans have what animals do not: the ability to choose between right and wrong. My dog chooses between comfort and discomfort and pain and pleasure, but he has no ability to decide what's best for my family. So I'm grateful that I'm to rule over *him* and not vice versa.

We must rule gently, of course. Our position over animals does not give us permission to abuse or neglect them. Our position over animals is a matter of stewardship.

You and I—not Gator and Cooper—are made in the image of God.

You and I are carriers of the life breath of God.

You and I are not animals, so we must not act like animals. Unlike animals, we have self-control. We *can* stop speeding, cheating, stealing, gazing at pornography, gambling away our family's money, watching inappropriate movies, listening to foul lyrics, exaggerating our accomplishments, and lying in bed next to someone other than a spouse. We must exercise self-control because it's part of who we are.

We must live dignified lives.

We must control our hands, minds, eyes, feet, and hearts.

We are not animals! And we must reject any implication or suggestion that we are.

I reject the theory of evolution for many reasons.

I reject evolution because I think it is bad science that's not supported by the physical evidence we find in and on this planet.

I reject evolution because I believe that God spoke this universe—and everything in it—into life in six twenty-four-hour days.

I reject evolution because I know who I am, and I don't want to think too lowly of myself.

I reject evolution because I know how dogs greet each other, and I know that I prefer to be human, shake hands, and say "God bless you."

QUESTIONS ABOUT WHO YOU ARE

FOR PERSONAL STUDY AND REFLECTION: *Before beginning this study, take some time to think about a former pet or a current pet—focusing on your pet's most interesting or extraordinary attributes. If you have a pet now, work through these questions with your pet in your lap, in the room, or next to the park bench on which you're sitting.*

FOR GROUP STUDY AND DISCUSSION: *Ask your group members to bring pictures of their pets, something that belongs to their pets, or their actual pets (if your group's meeting place is conducive to this). Begin this study by asking each group member to share something interesting about these pets (per questions 2 and 3). Then work through the other questions and Scriptures together.*

1. Did you have a pet when you were growing up? What was your pet's name? What's your favorite memory about that pet?

2. Do you have a pet now? What kind of pet is it? What's your pet's name? What do you like most about your pet?

3. They say that pets often look like their owners. Can you think of two ways you and your pet are alike? two ways you are different?

4. In the later 1700s, Carl Linnaeus, a Swedish botanist, physician, ecologist, and zoologist said: "I demand of you, and of the whole world, that you show me a generic character . . . by which to distinguish between Man and

Ape. I myself most assuredly know of none."[2] What is one thing that distinguishes man from ape?

_____

Read Genesis 1–3

_____

5. Choose three examples from this passage that show the power of God.

6. Choose three examples from this passage that show the love of God.

7. Choose three examples from this passage that show the nature of man.

8. How should the fact that we were deliberately created impact how we live?

9. What is one thing you can do this week to prove that you are not an animal but a human being made in the image of God?

"Lord, thank you for reminding me that I'm not an animal. I thank you that I am a human being—made in your image, blessed by you, and entrusted by you with the task of caring for this planet and everything on it."

YOU ARE GOD'S MASTERPIECE

Ruth and Chopin's Ballade in G Minor

The Lord God formed the man from the dust of the ground and breathed into his nostrils the breath of life, and the man became a living being.

GENESIS 2:7

We are God's masterpiece. He has created us anow in Christ Jesus, so that we can do the good things he planned for us long ago.

EPHESIANS 2:10, NLT

I need to explain to you why I cried while Ruth played Chopin on the piano in her living room. But first let me tell you about my mom's porcelain figurine of an old Japanese man.

I used to look at the old man and wish he could whisper some of the wonders he had witnessed on his journey to the top of our stereo.

I would look at his face, which wore a pleasant expression, and wonder. I was fascinated with the detail in his clothing, the intricacy of the artwork, and the way his gnarled hands and bony feet looked real. In fact, the little porcelain Japanese man looked so real, it seemed that—if he so wished—he could stretch out his skinny, old leg with its bony, bare foot to the polished, dark wood of the stereo cabinet and then, once sure-footed, slowly walk away. The porcelain Japanese man was frozen in a moment that appeared to be part of a precious memory of the Japanese artist who had created him. I found this porcelain Japanese figurine beautiful and captivating.

My grandparents had brought the figurine back from their visit to Japan as a gift for my mom. It was a very valuable and beautiful heirloom that would be passed down to one of us.

It was a reflection of both the love of an artist for art and the love of my grandparents for Mom. Each time Mom noticed the little Japanese man with the pleasant expression on his face, she was reminded that she was in her parents' thoughts—bringing a pleasant expression to *their* faces—even when they'd been on the other side of the world. My grandparents were now gone, so the figurine was an even more precious physical reminder of the love between Mom and her parents.

Mom displayed the porcelain man proudly on the stereo cabinet in the living room, where he sat silently, beautifully, and safely for many years . . . until one Thursday night in June.

My family likes to be together. We also like to have kids; so whenever we get together—at least at this stage in our lives—wherever the whenever is, children are everywhere.

My family and my sister's family were gathered at Mom's house to hang out and enjoy each other's company. The kids were playing, and no one was crying—or bleeding profusely—so we figured that everything was OK. And it was . . . until we heard a loud crash on the hardwood floor in the living room.

Leslie called out, "Kendall, where are you?"

We heard baby talk coming from the living room.

Kendall, my sister's youngest daughter, was only one-and-a-half at the time. She had been exploring in the living room—by herself—when she decided to play with the little porcelain man. He had fallen out of Kendall's tiny hands and met with the hardwood floor. As we rounded the corner, we found Kendall surrounded by a million tiny pieces of oriental porcelain. The barefooted Japanese man never had a chance.

Mom gasped but did not cry or do anything to make Kendall feel bad.

It was an *accident,* not an incident, so Mom graciously began picking up the pieces as she smiled and mumbled something about finding someone who might be able to put them back together again.

Kendall did nothing wrong. She was not being mean or disobedient. She wasn't being crafty. She was being one-and-a-half, so we cleaned up the mess and moved on.

One-and-a-half-year-old little girls and

> **I picture the Creator at his workbench with his bifocals on the end of his nose and a paintbrush poised in his right hand.**

porcelain Japanese men with bony toes, gnarled fingers, and pleasant expressions on their faces are not a good combination.

Each time I remember that incident—I mean, that *accident*—I think about us.

Each human being is a beautiful and valuable work of art.

I picture the Creator at his workbench with his bifocals on the end of his nose and a paintbrush poised in his right hand. In his other hand, he carefully holds us, one by one, wondering whether—based on the shape of our faces and the tones of our skin—our eyes should be blue, brown, or a light shade of green.

You and I are God's masterpieces, designed precisely and wonderfully by the master artist. I think of that each time I remember the dropped figurine—because I've seen what Satan has tried to do to so many of us.

How many times has God heard the crash and rounded the corner, only to find Satan standing amid the shattered pieces of the life of one of God's precious works of art?

Satan and humans are not a good combination.

God was busy touching up the universe, and there was no crying or profuse bleeding, so he figured everything was OK with his children.

> ## As he rounded the corner in the garden, he found Satan standing amid the shattered pieces of Adam's and Eve's souls.

He had been clear about the rules: "You are free to eat from any tree in the garden; but you must not eat from the tree of the knowledge of good and evil, for when you eat of it you will surely die" (Genesis 2:16, 17). He knew something had gone wrong when he heard the loud crash of human innocence as it fell in the garden that day.

God called out, "Where are you?" (Genesis 3:9).

As he rounded the corner in the garden, he found Satan standing amid the shattered pieces of Adam's and Eve's souls.

This was not how it was supposed to be. The human race had a chance. God designed us to live, not die.

He designed us to be good, not bad.

He designed us to be cherished, not destroyed.

He designed us to be admired, not ridiculed.

He designed us to be a reflection of his love, not of Satan's hate.

He designed us to live life with a pleasant expression on our faces.

He—God—designed us.

We are his workmanship. We are works of art.

Do you realize that you are God's masterpiece—and that God wants to enjoy you, but Satan wants to destroy you?

What you see when you look in the mirror is important.

Do you see a precious work of art, or do you see an accident?

Do you see a masterpiece or a piece of trash?

YOU ARE NOT AN ACCIDENT

Accidents happen when people aren't being careful.

Accidents happen when people are negotiating business deals on their cell phones instead of focusing on negotiating a safe change of lanes.

Accidents happen when people are late, rushed, stressed, and angry.

Accidents happen when people are being lazy.

When my wife and I moved back to Florida after graduate school, we rented a small house in the country. Mowing two acres with a push mower was rapidly eroding my love for living in the country; so we invested in a riding mower, which I kept in the carport, covered by a tarp held down by four paint cans.

One day I was rushing and being lazy at the same time, which is never a good combination. Instead of removing the tarp and folding it neatly beneath the four paint cans like I usually did, I hastily yanked one end of the tarp off the mower and flipped it to one side. I'd forgotten about the paint can that was behind the right rear tire of the mower. By the time I remembered, it was too late.

Red paint exploded all over me, the mower, and the carport.

It wasn't just red paint. It was red *oil-based* paint that seemed to spread everywhere as I desperately tried to clean it up with the garden hose. (Did I tell you that I was renting this house?)

Isn't it ironic that instances of laziness can so often lead to accidents that so often lead to hours of work?

Accidents happen when drunk men drive home.

Accidents happen when laws are broken.

Accidents happen when a little boy asks his friends, "Wanna see something cool?"

> **Accidents happen. But you and I didn't just happen. We were purposed. We were created.**

Accidents happen when one-and-a-half-year-old girls play with porcelain.

Accidents happen. But you and I didn't just happen. We were purposed. We were created. We each are a dream come true.

Paul, writing to Christians who were struggling with being mature and pure in a corrupt environment, reminds us, "We are God's masterpiece. He has created us anew in Christ Jesus, so that we can do the good things he planned for us long ago" (Ephesians 2:10, *NLT*). Paul wanted the Christians in Ephesus and beyond to realize that they didn't just happen. God has a specific job he wants each person to do, and he creates each one specifically to do that job.

No, you and I didn't just happen.

There was no "Oops."

No "I guess that will work."

We weren't accidents. When God looked at his plan and saw a need, he reached into the moist earth and began fashioning you and me into tools that would meet that need.

YOU ARE VALUABLE

Helen Frankenthaler's *The Bay* is an abstract painting on display in the Detroit Institute of Arts. It's valuable. This work of art is worth about 1.5 million dollars. Or I should say, it *used* to be worth 1.5 million dollars, until a twelve-year-old boy on a field trip decided that *The Bay* was the place to put his piece of Wrigley's Extra Polar Ice gum.

The gum left a stain the size of a quarter on the painting.

The boy was suspended from school and disciplined by his parents.

Following his suspension, Julie Kildee, the director of the boy's charter school, said, "Even though we give very strict guidelines on proper behavior and we hold students to high standards, he is only 12 and I don't think he understood the ramifications of what he did before it happened, but he certainly understands the severity of it now."[1]

Where the boy once saw something equivalent to the underside of a cafeteria table, he now sees a valuable piece of art.

We don't always understand the ramifications of what we do to our lives because we don't always understand how valuable we really are.

YOU ARE CREATED BY GOD

You are valuable because you were created by God. In Genesis 2:7 we read that God "formed" Adam. The Hebrew word used there is the same word used to describe how a potter fashions moist clay into a beautiful vase through an intricate process of shaping, squeezing, spinning, and heating the clay. God formed us into priceless pieces of art. We are not here *as* accidents or *by* accident. We existed in the mind of the master Creator before we existed in the womb. We reflect God's image, his power, his creativity, his goodness, and his love. We are to be cherished and admired.

In the opening chapter of his book *Natural Theology,* William Paley, a nineteenth-century Anglican philosopher, offers a powerful argument for God, now called the Watchmaker Argument, based on the intricate order we see in nature. Paley's analogy is a convincing argument for the power of God and the value of you. Paley wrote:

> In crossing a heath, suppose I pitched my foot against a stone, and were asked how the stone came to be there, I might possibly answer, that for any thing I knew to the contrary, it had

lain there for ever: nor would it perhaps be very easy to [show] the absurdity of this answer. But suppose I had found a watch upon the ground, and it should be inquired how the watch happened to be in that place, I should hardly think of the answer which I had before given, that, for any thing I knew the watch might have always been there. Yet why should not this answer serve for the watch, as well as for the stone? Why is it not as admissible in the second case, as in the first? For this reason, and for no other, viz., that, when we come to inspect the watch, we perceive (what we could not discover in the stone) that its several parts are framed and put together for a purpose. . . . This mechanism being observed . . . the inference, we think, is inevitable; that the watch must have had a maker; that there must have existed, at some time and at some place or other, an artificer or artificers who formed it for the purpose which we find it actually to answer; who comprehended its construction, and designed its use.[2]

It would be illogical to suggest that watches came into being without watchmakers, so it is illogical to think that we—who are a billion times more complex than my Timex Ironman 100 lap memory watch—came into existence as the eventual result of a big bang.

The brain shows great design. The human brain is the most complex organ in the human body, containing one hundred billion electrical connections (neurons), which is more than all the electrical connections in all the electrical appliances in the world.[3]

Our eyes show great design. The human eye is an incredibly complex organism whose design has mystified and amazed scientists like Charles Darwin for centuries. Of the human eye, Darwin wrote, "To suppose that the eye with all its inimitable contrivances for adjusting the focus to different distances, for admitting different amounts of light, and for the correction of spherical and chromatic aberration, could have been formed by natural selection, seems, I freely confess, *absurd in the highest degree*."[4] (emphasis added)

Even the human heart, as fragile as it appears to be, is designed so well that this 10-ounce pump will operate without maintenance or lubrication for about seventy-five years.

Our bodies show great design because we were created by the Great Designer. We are valuable.

YOU ARE UNIQUE

You are valuable because you are unique. That's what makes art, art—its uniqueness among the multitudes of images we process each day. The *Mona Lisa* is a treasure because it is not a Polaroid picture of your Aunt Peggy. That's what captures your attention when you see it. That's what evokes emotions. That's what inspires you when you're in its presence. That's why you'll pay six dollars for adults and three dollars per child to tour the Detroit Institute of Arts. And that's why you'd be outraged that a twelve-year-old boy put a piece of gum on such a painting. Art doesn't just happen, and it doesn't just happen every day. It's a unique blessing—and that's exactly what you are.

Look at yourself.

> No one else in the entire world can do what you do, the way you can do it.

You're unique. You're worth a lot more than six dollars; you're priceless. Out of the roughly 6.5 billion people breathing on this planet right now, there is no one else exactly like you. No one else in the entire world can do what you do, the way you can do it. Your unique life experiences combined with your unique physical makeup combined with your unique soul make you a valuable—and unique!—instrument in God's plan for redeeming this world.

YOU WERE BOUGHT AT A HIGH PRICE

And . . . you are valuable because of what God was willing to pay for you. Helen Frankenthaler's painting is valuable not just because it represents an investment of time, talent, and inspiration. Helen Frankenthaler's painting is valuable not just because Helen Frankenthaler thinks it is valuable. No. Helen Frankenthaler's painting is also valuable because, apparently, someone somewhere is willing to pay 1.5 million dollars for it.

You and I are valuable too. We know that because God was willing to pay a high price for us.

In 1 Corinthians 6:19, 20 Paul reminds us: "Do you not know that your body is a temple of the Holy Spirit, who is in you, whom you have received from God? You are not your own; you were bought at a price. Therefore honor God with your body."

> You and I are valuable too. We know that because God was willing to pay a high price for us.

God paid for us with the life of Jesus. When we become followers of Jesus Christ, our bodies become temples of the Holy Spirit. Our bodies are priceless works of art, not worthless pieces of trash. We're supposed to honor God with our bodies.

YOU ARE BEAUTIFUL

Sam was a fourteen-year-old purebred Chinese crested hairless who won the World's Ugliest Dog contest 2003–2005. Sam is covered in blackheads. His skin is wrinkled, brown, and dotted with splotches and several lines of warts. His eyes are pale and frightening. His teeth are misshapen and jut out of his mouth at odd angles. He has two hairs on his tail and five hairs on his head. He is so ugly that the judges at his first competition recoiled in horror when he was placed before them. But none of this seems to faze his owner, Susie Lockhee. In an interview on CBS's *The Early Show,* Lockhee said, "People who don't know him are pretty horrified. They're very horrified that I'm always kissing him. I'm very affectionate with Sammy because I think he's very beautiful. Beauty is definitely in the eye of the beholder, isn't it?"[5]

This is not just true for Sam; it is also true for us. Beauty *is* in the eye of the beholder, and we are "beheld" by God.

It's as if he has your picture in his wallet, which he regularly opens and then asks the nearest person, "Have you seen my boy? Good looking, isn't he?"

Or he has your picture on his fireplace mantle, and as he welcomes each guest to his living room, he pulls your picture from its special place and asks, "Have I shown you the picture of my beautiful girl?"

When he pulls down the sun visor in his car, your picture falls into his lap. And as he picks it up to look at it, he thinks to himself, *I love that kid.*

God adores you.

People who don't feel loved hurt themselves. A study in the *British Medical Journal* found that of the six thousand fifteen- and sixteen-year-old students they studied, 13 percent of them have "carried out an act of deliberate self-harm."[6] Why would teenagers cut themselves? They feel ugly and worthless.

People who don't feel beautiful go to great lengths to try to change themselves. I'm not talking about a diet, a new haircut, or joining a Pilates class. No, I'm talking about those people who feel so worthless that they try to seize control of their "failing" bodies through plastic surgery, metabolic steroids, binging, purging, and even starving. These are all attempts to combat feelings of insecurity and worthlessness.

A couple of years ago I received an e-mail from a young woman I'd met who is struggling with anorexia. Here's an insightful section from her e-mail: "I don't think others would really care if I was here or not. I'm sure some people would be thinking how it's best that I'm gone so I won't cause any more problems or be a burden to others. I am sure they can and probably will, but it seems like my life cannot get any worse. *I feel flawed and damaged.* The things that I really want out of life, I don't see happening. *Who is ever going to want someone who is so messed up and damaged?* I hate how I dread the future." (emphasis added)

Can you hear what she's really saying? This young woman feels worthless. When she looks in the mirror, she's not seeing a masterpiece. She's seeing mistakes, or more accurately, she's seeing what she thinks is one big mistake.

But she is not a mistake.

You are not a mistake.

You are not worthless!

If your father told you that, he's a liar.

If your mother told you that, she doesn't know what she's talking about.

If your boss tells you that, quit.

If your girlfriend tells you that you are worthless, dump her.

If your spouse tells you that you are worthless . . . then you sit him down, pull out your Bible, turn to Psalm 139, and proclaim the words of King David: "[God] created my inmost being; [he] knit me together in my mother's womb. I praise [God] because I am fearfully and wonderfully made; [his] works are wonderful, I know that full well" (vv. 13, 14).

If anyone tells you that you are worthless, don't just ignore him; confront him—because to ascribe no worth to yourself is to put spit-covered gum smack-dab in the middle of a masterpiece.

You are valuable and a priceless work of art, even if that's not what you see when you look in the mirror today.

Now picture a slab of marble.

Put a slab of marble in front of a cook, and you end up with a counter.

Put a slab of marble in front of an architect, and you get a cornerstone.

Put a slab of marble in front of a historian, and you get a monument.

Put a slab of marble in front of my friend Dale, who owns a tile business, and you get a floor.

Put a slab of marble in front of Michelangelo, and you get something amazing. When Michelangelo looked at a particular piece of marble, he saw what ended up being his sculpture *Angel Holding a Candelabra.*[7]

Asked about how he created such beautiful artwork out of a simple marble slab, he said, "I saw the angel in the marble and carved until I set him free."[8]

When God looks at your life, he doesn't just see what you are; he also sees what you *can* be. You are his masterpiece—an "angel" in the making. He sees you as valuable and beautiful. He's always seen you this way; and he is always carving, trying to set you free from your misunderstandings about yourself. This must not be forgotten during the painful chiseling.

> **When God looks at your life, he doesn't just see what you are; he also sees what you *can* be.**

This is why I cried when Ruth played Chopin's *Ballade in G Minor* on her piano.

Ruth had begun playing the piano when she was only five years old and living in the Philippines. It was not long before her exceptional talent began to blossom and capture the attention of people outside her family. Only one year after starting to play the piano, Ruth won a talent show on TV. Her talent was recognized and admired. She was considered a child prodigy. At age nine Ruth joined a music conservatory and began playing the piano at events all around the Philippines and on TV. When she was only eleven years old, Ruth played for the First Lady of the Philippines, Imelda Marcos. At sixteen Ruth moved to the United States to study at The Juilliard School in New York.

Ruth is a piano virtuoso.

When Ruth was nine years old, her mom asked her to learn Chopin's *Ballade in G Minor.* Frederick Chopin, a nineteenth-century Polish composer, is credited with inventing ballades. Ballades are typically romantic and epic. Ballades are incredibly difficult to learn—and play—but Ruth, even though she was only nine, began to study her mom's favorite Chopin ballade. Over the next seven years, she dabbled with the song, but it wasn't until she studied this ballade at Juilliard at the age of seventeen with two different Polish piano masters that she finally learned how to play the difficult piece.

I was at a party at Ruth's house when Eli, Ruth's husband, asked her to play Chopin's *Ballade in G Minor.* Each person in the house fell silent as Ruth positioned herself carefully on the bench in front of her valuable and beautifully polished black, Yamaha, baby grand piano.

> Ruth played that piano like God wants to play us. That's why I cried.

As Ruth began to play, we all witnessed a merging of master and instrument.

For nearly fifteen minutes each of the almost fifty people in the house sat silent and motionless as Ruth played that piano as it was created to be played.

No key misplayed.

No movement wasted.

No note without purpose.

Ruth played that piano like God wants to play us.

That's why I cried.

I was overwhelmed by the music and by the perfect and powerful combination of master and instrument. But I began to cry because, as I watched and listened to Ruth play the piano, I realized that God created us to make beautiful music too. I saw God in Ruth, and I saw myself in that Yamaha, baby grand piano . . . and I saw you too.

I cried while Ruth played the piano because I saw an angel where before I saw only a slab of marble.

Like that piano, you and I are valuable and beautiful instruments—God's masterpieces—designed not for "Chopsticks," but for Chopin.

Remember this . . . and the next time Ruth plays Chopin's *Ballade in G Minor* on her piano, you'll cry too.

QUESTIONS ABOUT WHO YOU ARE

FOR PERSONAL STUDY AND REFLECTION: *When doing this study, have something you've created nearby (artwork, craft, poem, piece of furniture, model airplane, etc.). Or do this study in an art museum.*

FOR GROUP STUDY AND DISCUSSION: *Option 1) Ask all group members to bring something they created. Then begin this study with show-and-tell. Option 2) Ask each group member to bring his favorite piece of artwork from home. These options relate to questions 1 and 2. After answering those, discuss the remaining questions and read the Scriptures.*

1. Think about something you've created. Describe the steps you took to make your creation. What made you proud of it when you were finished? How did people react to your creation?

2. What is one of your favorite pieces of artwork? How did you feel when you first saw that piece of artwork? What do you like most about it?

3. If you could describe your life as a creative work, what kind would you be (painting, architecture, poem, sculpture, etc.)? Why?

4. Recall a time when you most felt like a valuable and beautiful piece of God's workmanship and a time when you didn't. What was the difference?

5. Just as Ruth played Chopin's *Ballade in G Minor* on her piano, God desires to interact with us and make beautiful music through our lives. If God were to play a song through your life right now, what song would we hear? Why?

_____

Read Genesis 1:26, 27; 2:7; Ephesians 2:10
_____

6. What is one of your favorite things about being human? What is one of your least favorite things about being human?

7. When you look in the mirror, what do you like best about yourself? What do you like least? How should the fact that we are God's masterpieces impact what we see when we look in the mirror?

8. When do you feel most valuable? most attractive?

9. What is one thing you can do this week to demonstrate that you are God's masterpiece?

"Lord, thank you for reminding me that I'm your masterpiece and not an accident. Thank you for reminding me of how valuable and beautiful I really am in your eyes."

YOU ARE IMPERFECT

The bad call

3

The eyes of both of them were opened, and they realized they were naked; so they sewed fig leaves together and made coverings for themselves.

GENESIS 3:7

All have sinned and fall short of the glory of God.

ROMANS 3:23

Don asked, "Did I get it right?"

The answer changed his life.

Don Denkinger was in, arguably, the biggest game of his career.[1] It was game six of the 1985 World Series between the Kansas City Royals and the St. Louis Cardinals. It was the bottom of the ninth inning. St. Louis was leading 1–0 and was only three outs away from winning the World Series and defeating their I-70 rivals.

Rookie reliever Todd Worrell was pitching, and Jorge Orta was at bat for the Royals. Don Denkinger was working as the first-base umpire when Orta hit the ball between first and second base. Worrell moved over to cover first. Jack Clark fielded the ball and tossed it to Worrell, who was waiting on first. Clark's toss was a little behind Worrell, but he reached back and caught it anyway. Don Denkinger was in his position and called out decisively, "Safe!"

It seemed like a routine play until the replay revealed Todd Worrell's foot planted firmly on the bag, ball in glove, long before Kansas City's Jorge Orta's foot reached the bag.

One mistake changed his life forever. Can you relate?

Denkinger had made a bad call.

The Royals rallied to score two runs, winning the game and demoralizing the Cardinals. The Cardinals lost the World Series when they lost game seven, 11–0. The St. Louis Cardinals and their fans demonized Denkinger. The manager for the Cardinals, Whitey Herzog, told Denkinger that he was directly responsible for the Cardinals having to play game seven. Denkinger was publicly ridiculed, criticized, and even threatened with death.

Denkinger was a major league official for thirty-one years and regarded as one of the best officials in the history of the game. Even so, to this day many St. Louis fans still blame him for the Cardinals losing the 1985 World Series.

One mistake changed his life forever.

Can you relate?

We make mistakes. We aren't perfect. (Ironically, I just mistyped the word *perfect,* and my spell-check system automatically corrected it for me.)

Some mistakes are public, like Denkinger's, but some are born and die in the heart, never revealing themselves as sin or ourselves as sinners.

Paul is clear: "All have sinned and fall short of the glory of God" (Romans 3:23).

The question is not "Are we imperfect?" but, rather, "Is there any hope for us?"

The answer reveals why admitting we are imperfect is not an ending, but a beginning.

We are all sinners who fell and who continue to fall short of God's glory. But truth be told, we don't usually *fall* into sin—we jump. In fact, we often step back so we can get a running start!

My family used to live in the country. One day Kyle, the son of my neighbor across the dirt road, came over with a great story. Kyle told me that when he got home from school, he was sure that his dog, One Toe (called One Toe because a raccoon had bitten off all the toes on his right front paw, except one, when he was a puppy), had killed my cat. I knew my cat was OK because I had just seen Snow Flake alive and well only moments ago, but I was curious.

"What made you think One Toe had killed my cat?" I asked.

"Well, he was covered in blood and guts—and he stunk somethin' fierce," Kyle explained, "so I thought he had killed your cat."

> **We don't usually *fall* into sin—we jump. In fact, we often step back so we can get a running start!**

This was getting good!

Kyle continued, "But he hadn't killed your cat. He'd been rollin' in a cow."

Kyle's family owned almost a thousand head of cattle. Occasionally, cows die in the field, and rarely are their bodies discovered until much later. Always, the hot Florida sun causes things to expand. One Toe, while out in the field, had come upon the bloated body of a dead cow, so he did what dogs do: he popped the bovine piñata, crawled into the animal's body cavity, and began rolling around in delight. The maggot-infested, deteriorating, rancid body of a cow had become Doggie Disneyland.

So when Kyle, One Toe's master, came home from school and found One Toe covered in cow, he was disgusted. Kyle could not abide One Toe's presence; he was covered in slime and he smelled.

As Kyle continued to describe how disgusting One Toe was, without knowing it he began to speak about me.

Too often when I enter the Lord's presence for corporate worship with other Christians on a Sunday morning, I do so stained by sin. How many Sundays do we come before the Holy One with a piece of Saturday night's sin still hanging from our spirits? How many evenings do we sit down to be intimate with God but are covered in the stench of a day's worth of sin?

> Do you have a hard time answering honestly when someone asks, "How are you doing?"

Kyle's only hope was in washing One Toe, so he got as much distance between himself and his dog as he could and turned on the hose. Only after that could Kyle truly embrace One Toe properly.

My only hope is in being washed too, but that would require that I admit I need a bath, which would require my admitting that I'm not perfect, which would require that I admit I am a sinner.

Which I am.

Disappointed? (You may want to close this book now, return it to the bookstore, and ask for your money back because the author, a minister, is not perfect. Or you may just want to read on.)

Do you have a hard time answering honestly when someone asks, "How are you doing?"

Two questions in the history of questions provoke more dishonesty than all others. The first is "Honey, do you think I've gained weight?" And the second is "How are you doing?" Answering these questions honestly can ruin a perfectly good day, conversation, and relationship; so being gripped by fear, we answer, "No, of course not" and "Fine," hoping that a nice smile will work as a distraction.

At some point we learn to play the Never Tell game (meaning, never tell anyone your problems, fears, concerns, doubts, or shortcomings because if they really know that you aren't perfect, then they won't like you). I don't know when it happens, but it's happened to everyone I know. My six-year-old son hasn't yet learned how to play the game. I ask him, "How are you doing, Levi?" And he will spend the next thirty minutes telling me—in great detail—exactly how he's doing. He'll tell me that he's doing great because he finally caught the lizard that has been hiding underneath the couch; or that he's not doing well because his sister won't share her crayons; or he's still sad that his fish, Superhero, went to swim in Heaven's crystal sea by way of the porcelain portal.

Levi is still authentic with me because he hasn't been hurt from telling people his problems, fears, concerns, doubts, and shortcomings only to have them use his confession against him. Inevitably, he *will* be hurt. Then he'll stop being authentic, and the Never Tell game will begin. Levi is honest with me now—in his innocence he doesn't realize that it's not OK for people to be imperfect.

Admitting we are imperfect is not an ending, but a beginning.

THE BLESSING OF ADMITTING WE'RE NOT PERFECT

Admitting imperfection is a double-edged sword. The blessing we receive by admitting that we aren't perfect is healing. Alcoholics Anonymous, by requiring authenticity, has been unbelievably successful in healing people who struggle with alcohol addiction. Each AA meeting begins with members confessing, "My name is Joe, and I am an alcoholic." "My name is Beth, and I am an alcoholic." "My name is _____, and I'm an alcoholic." This is a difficult but essential confession for anyone who truly wants to be healed. The mask must come off. The hypocrisy must end. The problem cannot be healed until the problem is confessed.

As a minister I deal with hurting people on a *weekly* basis. I deal with people who have a *weakly* basis. I too have a *weakly* basis.

I anticipate our Sunday morning services for many reasons, not the least of which is the opportunity for people to get real with each other and with God. But inauthenticity happens every week despite our best intentions. Each Sunday in our church and in churches around the world, Christians wake up with the same serious problems that non-Christians have. Determined to persevere, they get ready, drive to church, park their cars, and resume the game. The I-don't-have-a-care-in-the-world-because-I'm-perfect mask goes on before they get out of their cars; and as they walk through the doors of the church, the game begins.

> As a minister I deal with hurting people on a *weekly* basis. I deal with people who have a *weakly* basis.

If I could, I would start each Sunday morning worship service by requiring every member to stand and get real.

"My name is Mike, and I'm afraid of losing my job."

"My name is LaVonda, and I can't pay my bills."

"My name is Jennifer, and I don't understand why my teenage daughter won't talk to me."

"My name is Adam, and I'm afraid I'm going to die."

"My name is Teresa, and I don't like myself."

"My name is Javier, and I have no idea how to be a good father because my dad left us when I was five."

"My name is Lori, and my heart is broken."

"My name is Peter, and I'm depressed."

"My name is Sachi, and my husband just left me for another woman."

"My name is Robert, and I'm addicted to pornography."

"My name is Meg, and I hate working in the nursery. I was afraid to tell you all because I don't want you to think I'm a bad person."

"My name is Arron, and I want you to like me."

Since we are imperfect humans living in a fallen world, we all eventually encounter pain, problems, failures, doubt, and fear. We can choose to deny life's problems and hide them behind a forced smile, a wink, and empty words like: "I'm doing great. How 'bout you?" "Couldn't be better!" "Can't complain." Or we can get real and admit that since we are not God, we could use some help.

There is true power in admitting that we are not perfect. Authentic people are powerful people. Take my favorite superhero, Superman, for example. I think we forget that Superman pretended to be Clark Kent and not vice versa. If Clark Kent were to be authentic and show the world who he really was all of the time, then he would have been extremely conspicuous in any situation except a costume party—because he would have been wearing tights, a cape, and a big *S* on his chest. Clark Kent was a disguise Superman wore to hide who he really was. At just the right time, Superman would take off his Clark Kent disguise so that he could do what he was born to do: save the world. He was forced to wear his Clark Kent costume because people were not ready to accept him for who he really was. Wearing the Clark Kent costume actually protected him against constant attack from his enemies, but it also concealed his true identity.

Our true identity is that we are all beautiful creations of God, designed by God for a special purpose. You and I were called to work with God and, in his power, help the people of this world find salvation through Jesus Christ. We don't have to be perfect; we just have to be available. We don't have to leap tall buildings in a single bound; we just have to walk past our insecurities. We don't have to stand face-to-face with a villain;

we just have to face our fears and trust in God's power to protect us as we fight to reach those who are entrapped in Satan's snares.

Everyone needs saving. It's time for Christians to get real. We must take off our mild-mannered-Clark-Kent-I-have-no-problems-so-let-me-just-blend-in costumes and experience the power of wearing our true identity. Then we'll be the super-people God planned for us to be . . . imperfections and all.

> Why can't we just admit that we're not God, so we're not perfect, so what you see is what you get, and that's OK?

Those who admit that they are imperfect are not wasting power on pretending, sneaking, hiding, and running, so they have more power to apply to living. One of my goals as a minister is to help people understand that it's a colossal waste of time and energy to play identity games with each other. Why can't we just admit that we're not God, so we're not perfect, so what you see is what you get, and that's OK? Too many Christians are missing the blessing of authenticity because they have bought into the lie that it's un-Christian to struggle on any level.

But it's not un-Christian to have problems.

It's not un-Christian to hurt.

It's not un-Christian to struggle with sin.

It's not un-Christian to have a difficult marriage.

It's not un-Christian to make mistakes while raising children.

It's not un-Christian to hate your job.

It's not un-Christian to be afraid to die.

It's not un-Christian if sometimes we are even afraid to live.

We are not God!

I am not God! There is power is this confession. I'm not always a good husband. Sometimes I make bad decisions as a father. Sometimes—

OK, often—I sin. I regularly get in trouble because I speak before I think. I'm a little insecure. Sometimes my breath stinks. I did some stupid stuff in high school. I get mad when someone cuts me off in traffic. I don't always answer the phone; I have caller ID, and there are some people I don't want to talk to. And occasionally I speed on my way to church. There, I said it!

I know it seems to be counterintuitive, but you and I are more powerful when we admit that we are sometimes weak. You and I are more courageous when we admit that we're sometimes scared to death. And you and I are closer to Christ's perfection when we are honest enough to admit that—unlike Christ—we aren't perfect.

THE CURSE OF ADMITTING WE'RE NOT PERFECT

The curse of admitting that we are not perfect is that there is the potential of pain. When we expose our hearts to others, we make ourselves more vulnerable. Authenticity involves risk. I have to tell you that it is a lot safer playing the game and never truly revealing to anyone who you really are. If you decide to get real, you are most likely going to get hurt somewhere by someone. Authentic, imperfect people make themselves targets for ridicule, judgment, and shame.

A transparent, imperfect life is not for cowards. Authentic people know the pain of having secrets—entrusted to a friend discretely— shouted mockingly by an enemy for all to hear; of tears, spilled in sorrow to a loved one, brought back to try to drown you in shame by one seeking

Hurt people hurt people.

revenge; and of freely sharing your true self with the hope of finally being accepted, only to have your true self ridiculed and rejected by heartless critics. Hurt people hurt people. Openly imperfect people are often attacked by delusional imperfect people who think that they are perfect and find it easier to criticize flaws in others than to deal with their own imperfections.

But openly imperfect people also know that the healing and liberation found only in authenticity are worth the risk of being hurt.

I remember a day I fell off my bike while racing down a gravel road, opening several large wounds on the left side of my body. It took about an hour for my friend Matt's mom to clean the dirt and gravel out of those wounds. It hurt, but I knew it was the best thing to do.

The next morning I had a soccer game. My wounds were bandaged and somewhat forgotten until I slid in the dirt to kick the ball, ripping off the bandages, and filling every wound once again with dirt. I went to the sideline, re-covered my dirty wounds with fresh bandages, and continued to play the game.

> Some of us are walking around with wounds that will not heal, simply because we—out of the fear of pain—refuse to reveal them to anyone.

After the game my dad took me out to the picnic table in the backyard. Slowly and carefully Dad removed each bandage, exposing my wounds to the air. Then he began to clean them. Each wound was covered in dirt, and I cried as my dad scrubbed away the dirt from the raw wounds. The pain was excruciating. To this day I can still hear my dad whispering, "I'm so sorry, son. I know this hurts, but your wounds won't heal properly unless I get all the dirt out." I made myself vulnerable to my dad because I knew that he had the best intentions. I endured the pain because I wanted to be healed. Hurt was the price I paid for healing.

Some of us are walking around with wounds that will not heal, simply because we—out of the fear of pain—refuse to reveal them to anyone. God's Word clearly teaches us that healing is found in acknowledging that we are imperfect.

In 1 John 1:8, 9 we read, "If we claim to be without sin, we deceive ourselves and the truth is not in us. If we confess our sins, he is faithful and just and will forgive us our sins and *purify* us from all unrighteousness." (emphasis added) Now, admitting our imperfections, our sins, to God may not be a pleasant experience. In fact, it may be a very painful ordeal, but John leaves no room for doubt—only in confession to God do we find forgiveness and purification.

> We need to find a way to be open and honest about our imperfections with *somebody.*

In James 5:16 we read, "Confess your sins to each other and pray for each other so that you may be *healed.*" (emphasis added) I'm fairly positive that confessing our sins to each other may not be a pleasant experience. In fact, I'm pretty sure that it might be a very, very painful and risky ordeal, but James plainly points out that only in authenticity with each other do we find true healing.

However, here's a word of caution: I don't think this Scripture indicates that we need to stand up in front of the church on Sunday morning and confess every rotten thing we've ever done. First of all, church gatherings in New Testament times were more intimate and, therefore, conducive to confession among friends. I believe this Scripture teaches us that we must design opportunities within today's church for the safe and discreet confession of sin. It's clear that God expects us to confess our sins to each other. But this must be done carefully and prayerfully. There are some people who are mature enough to handle your confession of sins, but there are some who are not. I don't recommend opening up and confessing our sins to everybody, but I believe—if we want to be faithful to God—we need to find a way to be open and honest about our imperfections with *somebody.*

Think of a scenario in which you admit your imperfections. It may resemble a bad dream. You know the one—the anxiety dream in which you're at school and you're naked and everyone is pointing at you, laughing, and there's nothing you can do to hide your . . . flaws.

We all have them. Flaws, that is. But that hasn't always been the case. Once upon a time we humans were flawless—alive and naked in the world, but we didn't know we were, so we didn't care that we were. Adam and Eve were perfect—not God, but good. They were so pure that they didn't feel guilt or shame at wearing no clothes. Our nightmare was their reality, and they didn't care because they didn't know anything better—all they knew *was* better. Unlike us, they had a better world, better health, better life, better dreams, and a better relationship with God; that is, until they gave in to temptation and gave up their perfection.

After accepting Satan's offer and eating the forbidden fruit from the tree of the knowledge of good and evil, everything changed. Moses records, "Then the eyes of both of them were opened, and they realized they were naked; so they sewed fig leaves together and made coverings for themselves" (Genesis 3:7).

> Our awareness—and admission—of our imperfection signifies a beginning.

That's why admitting we are imperfect is not an ending, but a beginning.

Adam and Eve's realization that they were not perfect was the beginning of the end for them, but our realization of our own imperfection is the *end of the beginning* for us. The moment Adam and Eve realized they were imperfect was the moment they realized that they were sinners who were not going to live forever. But on this side of the cross of Jesus Christ, the moment we realize—and admit—that we are imperfect sinners who will not live forever without Jesus Christ is the moment that signifies the end of the first phase of our justification.

Adam and Eve's awareness of their imperfection signified an ending.

Our awareness—and admission—of our imperfection signifies a beginning.

Are we imperfect? Yes.

Is there any hope for us? Yes.

Today, if you go to Don Denkinger's house, you can see a picture of "the bad call." Denkinger has purchased, enlarged, and framed a picture of himself making the bad call during the bottom of the ninth inning in game six of the 1985 World Series. And he's hung it—not in a back closet in a back room, but in a place where everyone can see it. The picture shows what really happened and that Denkinger was wrong; yet he still displays it prominently in his den.

He keeps it as a reminder that no one's perfect.

And he's right.

But that's not the ending; it's the beginning.

QUESTIONS ABOUT WHO YOU ARE

FOR PERSONAL STUDY AND REFLECTION: *Go to a local baseball diamond to do your personal study with these questions, or hold a baseball and a glove while you study and reflect.*

FOR GROUP STUDY AND DISCUSSION: *Start the group time by holding a baseball in a glove and confessing a mistake you've made in your life. Then toss the ball to someone else in the group. Whoever receives the ball is the next person to share. Proceed until everyone who is willing has had a chance to share a mistake he or she has made. This activity leads naturally into the questions.*

1. What are the first and second best decisions you've ever made? Why?

2. What is the first bad decision you remember making when you were young? What lessons did you learn from that mistake?

3. What is one of the worst decisions you've made in the past year? Why? What were the consequences?

4. In your opinion, what are some of the biggest reasons we make poor decisions?

Read Genesis 3:1-24

5. How did this event impact Satan? Eve? Adam? us?

6. What is your best definition of the word *sinner*?

Read Romans 3:23

---

7. Can you think of a defining moment at which you realized or thought that you were a sinner? How did you feel when you discovered this? What was your response?

8. How can you make the reminder that you are imperfect, a sinner, the beginning of something special?

9. What is one way this reminder will impact what you do this week?

"Lord, thank you for reminding me that I'm not perfect—and that I don't have to be. Please forgive me for the following specific sins: _____

_____ .

And help me embrace the idea of beginning again."

YOU ARE RIGHTEOUS
One small step

4

> *Noah was a righteous man, blameless among the people of his time, and he walked with God.*
>
> GENESIS 6:9

> *God made him who had no sin to be sin for us, so that in him we might become the righteousness of God.*
>
> 2 CORINTHIANS 5:21

On September 12, 1962, President John F. Kennedy delivered a speech at Rice University in Houston, Texas. The speech ignited something in the heart of this nation that drove men and women to do more and go further than we'd ever gone before. In his speech at Rice, President Kennedy made us believe that we could do more than we'd ever done before and be more than we ever imagined we could be.

President Kennedy said:

> We choose to go to the moon. We choose to go to the moon in this decade and do the other things, not because they are easy, but because they are hard, because that goal will serve to organize and measure the best of our energies and skills, because that challenge is one that we are willing to accept, one we are unwilling to postpone, and one which we intend to win, and the others, too. . . .

> I think we're going to do it, and I think that we must pay what needs to be paid. . . . It may be done while some of you are still here at school at this college and university. It will be done during the term of office of some of the people who sit here on this platform. But it will be done. And it will be done before the end of this decade.[1]

For the first time in our history, reaching the moon no longer seemed unattainable. The idea of a man walking on the moon was no longer a fantasy; it was an anticipated reality. Traversing the darkness of space no longer frightened us; it made us courageous. And although the moon hadn't moved, it was closer than it had ever been before.

President Kennedy was assassinated on November 22, 1963, a little more than a year after planting this speech in the heart of a generation. But his vision of sending a man to the moon before the end of the decade had been so compelling, it lived on. And the dream became a reality when Neil Armstrong touched his foot to the surface of the moon on July 20, 1969.

Man's walking on the moon changed everything we believed about ourselves and our potential. Neil Armstrong said, "That's one small step for a man, one giant leap for mankind."[2] We all realized that if Neil Armstrong—one of us, a man—could do something so big and courageous, we could too.

If President Kennedy's words changed how we looked at this world, Neil Armstrong's words changed how we walk through it. Post-July 20, 1969, we walked the surface of the earth knowing we could also walk on the surface of the moon if we decided to.

In one of my favorite movies of all time, *Apollo 13,* Jim Lovell (played by Tom Hanks), after watching Neil Armstrong walk on the moon, says to his wife, "From now on, we live in a world where man has walked on the moon. And it's not a miracle, we just decided to go."[3]

Man's walking on the moon changed everything we believed about ourselves and our potential.

Does the idea that you have the potential of being righteous seem out of this world? Does righteousness seem unattainable?

If the idea of your walking in the righteousness of God seems as unbelievable as the notion of your walking on the surface of the moon, read on. Noah was considered righteous, and if he, a normal guy, could be viewed as righteous, then there's hope for you and me. There's even hope for imperfect umpires like Don Denkinger.

The first time the word *righteous* is ever used in the Bible, it is used to define Noah: "Noah was a righteous man, blameless among the people of his time, and he walked with God" (Genesis 6:9). The word *righteous* is a "church word" that means "uprightness" or simply "right."

BLAMELESS

I hit the college campus my freshman year as the son of a professor, driving my own car (1972 green Ford Maverick) and wearing my Ray-Ban aviator sunglasses (the same kind worn by Tom Cruise in the most popular movie of that summer, *Top Gun*). I was the leader of the Arron Is Hot Stuff Club. I was also the sole member.

I'd arrived on campus with pretty low goals. As an eighteen-year-old, I didn't really go to college to learn; I went to college to play basketball and meet girls. I did well enough in my classes to stay out of trouble with Coach Chestnut and my dad, but not well enough to make any of those lists that are named after the most influential school administrators and guarantee that you get to wear those pretty gold cords around your neck at graduation.

I liked to make people laugh and often went to class with that as my goal for the day. In one class I decided that each day of the semester I would set the alarm on my watch to go off in the middle of class. I hid my watch in different places around the room (like inside my friends' backpacks), so that when the alarm sounded it always sounded from someplace else, directing attention to *someone* else. Eventually, I was the only one who thought this was funny.

> **The professor asked, "Who did this?" and the whole class pointed at me.**

Did I mention I was eighteen years old?

One day, bored with the alarm gag, I decided to try something a little more daring. I arrived at class early, set my alarm for 2:14 PM, and placed my watch in the overhead projector right next to the professor's podium. I took my seat, my classmates and professor arrived, and I waited in anticipation of fourteen minutes after two.

At 2:12 PM everything went wrong.

The professor turned on the overhead projector. The professor had *never* turned on the overhead projector, but that day he did. Thick, black smoke began to billow out of the machine as the rubber wristband on my watch melted on the projector bulb. As our mild-mannered professor turned into heroic fireman, I sat stunned while the rest of the class laughed heartily, realizing that, finally, the joke was going to be on me.

After hastily extinguishing the fire, the professor asked, "Who did this?" and the whole class pointed at me.

It was a humbling experience.

No one ever pointed at Noah when the teacher asked, "Who did this?"

Noah was righteous, blameless in a world full of guilty people. From where God was observing, everyone except Noah was to blame for the wickedness flourishing in the post-Eden world. Moses writes in Genesis 6:5-8: "The LORD saw how great man's wickedness on the earth had become, and that every inclination of the thoughts of his heart was only evil all the time. The LORD was grieved that he had made man on the earth, and his heart was filled with pain. So the LORD said, 'I will wipe mankind, whom I have created, from the face of the earth—men and animals, and creatures that move along the ground, and birds of the air—for I am grieved that I have made them.' But Noah found favor in the eyes of the LORD."

It's a profound truth: Righteous people shine brightest in the darkness . . . kind of like bright stars in a dark night sky.

Have you ever really seen the stars?

Working in Yellowstone National Park one summer gave me many opportunities to see the stars like I had never seen them. A dock on Yellowstone Lake, several hours from any ground lighting and from the nearest city, became my front-row seat to the galaxy that had been hidden in over-urbanized and over-lit Orlando, Florida.

From that dock, I was able for the first time to watch satellites move across the sky. I saw the Milky Way and understood how amazing God's promise to Abraham in Genesis 22:17 really was.

Last November my family and I were delivering Thanksgiving food baskets to families in need around central Florida. One of the families to whom we delivered a basket lived in a town about forty-five miles south of Orlando called Kenansville.

The best way to Kenansville from our house requires a long drive down a remote two-lane road through the middle of nowhere. On the way back, one of my sons commented that he couldn't believe how many stars he was seeing. Sensing a teachable moment, I pulled over as soon as I could. I turned off the headlights and ushered my family out of the car, into the darkness, and onto front-row seats for one of the greatest shows on earth. My kids oohed and aahed as they really saw for the very first time the stars in all their magnificence—as God created them to be seen.

Stars were made to shine in the darkness.

Stars were made to be seen and to testify of God's faithfulness to his promise to Abraham.

The constellations were made to be easily seen as artwork hanging in the gallery of the sky, testifying nightly to the existence of a master artist.

Stars were made to guide us on our mission and bring us home again.

I wish I could take you on a cloudless night to that dock on the south side of Yellowstone Lake or to that spot outside of Kenansville. You could see what I'm talking about—and what God expects to see when he lies on the dock and looks at this world.

> When blameless people shine, hopeless people have a bright light in a dark sky by which to find their way home.

When God looked at Noah's world, instead of seeing a multitude of righteous people, he saw only one soul shining in a vast darkness.

Righteous people are blameless, and blameless people shine. And when blameless people shine, hopeless people have a bright light in a dark sky by which to find their way home. Knowing this, Paul wrote to the Christians in Philippi: "Do everything without complaining or arguing, so that you may become blameless and pure, children of God without fault in a crooked and depraved generation, in which you shine like stars in the universe" (Philippians 2:14, 15).

Noah shone. Noah was righteous, and we can decide to be too. You and I were made to shine. We were not made to be blocked out by ground lighting and to be indiscernible from the infinite darkness by which we are surrounded in this fallen world. We can be blameless. Despite what we expect from ourselves, God has always expected us to be blameless.

Paul wrote, "He chose us in him before the creation of the world to be holy and blameless in his sight" (Ephesians 1:4).

Noah lived and died long before Christ's arrival as a baby in Bethlehem, so his blamelessness was not because of his faith in the death, burial, and resurrection of Christ, but in faithful obedience to God. Blamelessness on this side of the cross happens only in Christ, and being "in him" is our choice—but it's not our *only* choice. We can choose instead to be sinful, selfish, and evil. But if we choose that path, we are choosing to walk directly in the way of God's wrath and judgment, so we leave ourselves open to blame. You see, being blameless is not something we do; it is something we either are or are not. And whether we are or not isn't based on our own ideas about what blameless is. Our opinion as to our guilt is completely irrelevant and will be completely irrelevant when we are standing before the judge on Judgment Day.

Even though we may *feel* blameless, it is not until God views us as blameless that we truly have hope. And God will view us as blameless only when he sees that we are standing with faith in—and forgiven by—the blood of his Son, Jesus. Blamelessness begins with God, not us, and is found only in Christ, not in wishful thinking or a high opinion of ourselves. Only God's opinion really matters.

God, as the judge, has the right to decide who is, and who is not, guilty.

Star-likeness, for us, is not unreachable; it is our destiny and our potential reality through Jesus Christ. Speaking of Christ's ability and God's role in making us righteous, Paul wrote, "God made him who had no sin to be sin for us, so that in [Jesus] we might become the righteousness of God" (2 Corinthians 5:21).

God, knowing that we were guilty but desiring to give us a way out, pointed his finger at Jesus and said, "He did it!" Jesus is our Savior, but he was God's sacrifice to save us from our sins. It was God's decision, not ours, to make Jesus our Messiah; but it is our decision, not God's, whether or not we will make Jesus our Savior. And it is not until we make Jesus our Savior that we can be viewed as blameless.

Trying to explain this concept to Titus (and us), Paul wrote: "At one time we too were foolish, disobedient, deceived and enslaved by all kinds of passions and pleasures. We lived in malice and envy, being hated and hating one another. But when the kindness and love of God our Savior appeared, he saved us, not because of righteous things we had done, but because of his mercy. He saved us through the washing of rebirth and renewal by the Holy Spirit, whom he poured out on us generously through Jesus Christ our Savior" (Titus 3:3-6).

But being righteous is more than being blameless; it also requires us to be faithful.

A CONSISTENT WALK WITH GOD

Noah was not just blameless; he was faithful. And Noah's faithfulness is described as walking with God.

My dad was a tall man with long legs. When I was young, I had to take two steps to keep up with every one of his. I remember walking down the sidewalk at my dad's side, trying to match his strides . . . or following him, trying to step in his footprints. I didn't think that I'd ever be able to keep up with him, but as time passed and as I grew, eventually I was able to walk side by side and stride for stride with my father.

> It is not until we make Jesus our Savior that we can be viewed as blameless.

Noah walked with God, side by side and stride for stride.

Because Noah was a righteous man, God gave him and his family a choice—and a chance—to be saved. God told Noah that because of the wickedness on the earth, he was going to destroy the world and everyone in it. God told Noah to build an ark, he told him exactly how to build it, and he told him exactly how to fill it up. God was not asking Noah; he was commanding Noah, and Noah chose to obey.

Make sure you don't miss that point. Noah had a choice. Noah could have said, "Lord, I believe in you and I believe in your power and I believe that you are going to destroy the earth, but I'm not really feeling called to build an ark right now. The idea of spending the next hundred years working on a boat and then filling that boat with smelly animals and then floating around with those smelly animals for a year while the waters subside doesn't sound like it fits my area of giftedness. So if it's all the same to you, I'm going to pass on this construction project." And if Noah had said that (or something similar), he would have ceased to be righteous because righteousness requires faithful obedience. So it is not surprising that Moses notes Noah's faithfulness two times: "Noah did everything just as God commanded him" (Genesis 6:22) and "Noah did all that the LORD commanded him" (Genesis 7:5).

Because Noah was a righteous man, Noah walked side by side and stride for stride with God and did everything his Father told him to do.

WRONG THINKING ABOUT RIGHTEOUSNESS

We have a couple of misconceptions about righteousness.

The first is that we can *do* righteousness. We can't *do* righteousness. Righteousness comes by faith. Pointing to the flood event, the writer of Hebrews is clear when he says, "By faith Noah, when warned about things not yet seen, in holy fear built an ark to save his family. By his faith he condemned the world and became heir of the righteousness that comes by faith" (Hebrews 11:7).

We can't do enough good works to be considered righteous, but because we are righteous we must do good works. This is what James points out in James 2:14-24:

> What good is it, my brothers, if a man claims to have faith but has no deeds? Can such faith save him? Suppose a brother or sister is without clothes and daily food. If one of you says to him, "Go, I wish you well; keep warm and well fed," but does nothing about his physical needs, what good is it? In the

same way, faith by itself, if it is not accompanied by action, is dead.

But someone will say, "You have faith; I have deeds."

Show me your faith without deeds, and I will show you my faith by what I do. You believe that there is one God. Good! Even the demons believe that—and shudder.

You foolish man, do you want evidence that faith without deeds is useless? Was not our ancestor Abraham considered righteous for what he did when he offered his son Isaac on the altar? You see that his faith and his actions were working together, and his faith was made complete by what he did. And the scripture was fulfilled that says, "Abraham believed God, and it was credited to him as righteousness," and he was called God's friend. You see that a person is justified by what he does and not by faith alone.

In the same way, was not even Rahab the prostitute considered righteous for what she did when she gave lodging to the spies and sent them off in a different direction? As the body without the spirit is dead, so faith without deeds is dead.

The second misconception is that we can *don* righteousness. But righteousness is not something we wear; it's who we are. When I was growing up, I had "church clothes"—the ones I was allowed to wear only on Sundays. I was not permitted to play in them. If I wanted to play, I had to put on my "play clothes." If this was not confusing enough, I also had "school clothes." Apparently, they could help me learn in a way that my play clothes could not because I was never allowed to wear play clothes to school.

Christians can make dressing up on Sunday a standard for determining one's "righteousness." Maybe that's because clothes are easier to clean than lives. But I'd rather be with a bunch of holy Christians in holey jeans than with a bunch of unholy hypocrites in fancy clothes any day.

I believe that Christians should dress appropriately when we gather with the church body, but that shouldn't take the place of living appropriately as the church during the week.

God is not impressed with, or fooled by, our clothes. If we are living sinful lives and think we can hide that fact from God by donning silk suits or designer skirts, we haven't read Isaiah 64:6 recently. The prophet wrote, "All of us have become like one who is unclean, and all our righteous acts are like filthy rags; we all shrivel up like a leaf, and like the wind our sins sweep us away."

Noah's righteousness had nothing to do with what he was wearing, but with how—and with whom—he was walking.

Last summer, my family and I attended a convention in downtown Louisville, Kentucky. Our hotel was located several blocks away from the convention center, so we walked to and from the convention. One afternoon, as we were walking back so the kids and I could take the all-important afternoon naps, I noticed that my youngest son, Sylas, was walking next to me and trying to match my strides. He had to take two steps for every one of mine. He's only four, but he's growing. One day he will be walking with me—side by side and stride for stride—physically. But my prayer is that one day he will be walking with me spiritually too. That's the desire of this father's heart and of our Father's heart as well. The Lord longs for you and me to walk with him—full of faith and faithfully—through this life and for all eternity.

Lao Tzu, a Chinese philosopher, is credited with saying, "A journey of a thousand miles must begin with a single step."[4] You may feel that righteousness is a thousand miles away from where you are right now. Don't be discouraged. There is hope.

Righteousness is reachable, but you must decide to move toward it.

And take heart. You don't have to build an ark or make a giant leap . . . a small step toward Jesus will do.

QUESTIONS ABOUT WHO YOU ARE

FOR PERSONAL STUDY AND REFLECTION: *If possible, do this study at night beneath a starry sky. Use a telescope or binoculars to look at the stars in moments of reflection.*

FOR GROUP STUDY AND DISCUSSION: *If it's possible to do this study on a starry night, secure the use of a telescope or binoculars. Start the discussion by giving each group member an opportunity to look at the stars close-up. Ask everyone to reflect on what they saw. Then proceed with the questions and Scriptures.*

1. Noah was described as righteous. What is the most common adjective used to describe you? Why?

2. What do you *wish* was the most common adjective used to describe you? Why?

3. What two words best describe your relationship with God now?

Read Genesis 6:9

4. Fill in the blanks so that Genesis 6:9 applies to you at this point in your spiritual walk: This is the account of _____ _____ *(your name).* _____ *(your name)* was a _____ *(adjective)* man/woman, _____ *(adjective)* among the people of his/her time, and he/she _____ *(verb, past tense)* with God.

Read Romans 5:18, 19

5. Which "one trespass" led to our condemnation?

6. What "one act of righteousness" brings life for all people?

7. How was Christ obedient? Did he have a choice?

8. What is the only thing that can make us righteous in the eyes of God?

9. What thoughts come to mind as you consider the idea of your life shining like a star?

10. What is one specific way you could walk in step with God this week?

"Lord, when people reflect on my life after I am gone, I want them to remember me as a shining star, as righteous. I'm learning that doing what I think is right could be different from what you think is right. So today I decide that I will:

_____

_____

_____

_____ *."*

YOU ARE CHOSEN

"I'll take the tall, skinny guy with the bowl haircut."

5

The LORD your God has chosen you.

DEUTERONOMY 7:6

Jesus . . . saw two brothers. . . . They were fishermen. "Come, follow me," Jesus said.

MATTHEW 4:18, 19

You are a chosen people, . . . a people belonging to God, that you may declare the praises of him who called you out of darkness into his wonderful light.

1 PETER 2:9

It's no fun to be chosen last.

Did you ever have this experience on the playground at elementary school? A leader in the group decided on a game of kickball.

At this point some dark and powerful force took over, and the two most popular boys were chosen to be the most powerful people in the universe: captains. Then everyone else transformed into puppies in a pet store—trying to look cute so the nice people on the other side of the glass would like them, rescue them from a dark future stuck in the cage of unpopularity, and take them home to live happily ever after.

As the captains chose their respective teams, those yet to be chosen folded their arms, looked down, and shuffled their feet, with hopes that their names would be called sooner rather than later. In this process of choosing, the all-powerful captains determined the destiny and value of each member of the group, one by one—for the pending game and, possibly, for the foreseeable future on the playground.

"I'll take Billy."

"Give me Tyler."

"Joey."

"Brooke."

"David."

As the teams grew larger, the group of "unchosens" grew smaller and felt more conspicuous as they wondered when, or if, they would be selected.

"Maurice."

"Beth."

"Amy."

"Rob."

A young boy has four great fears on the playground:

1) getting beat up by the school bully,

2) getting chosen after a girl,

3) getting beat up by a girl on the playground,

4) and the greatest of all playground fears . . . getting picked last.

"I guess I'll take Arron."

It's no fun to be picked last. We think it means there is something wrong with us, or maybe we think there is something wrong with the captain, who considers some of us as only one step better than no one. We think it means that we are flawed. We think it means that our peers perceive us as having no value. We may even think it means we aren't wanted.

Take heart. No matter how many times you've been picked last by the people around you, you must always remember that you were picked first by the one who made you. And his opinion is the only one that matters.

Paul tells us that before we were even born, God chose us. To the Ephesians Paul wrote, "He chose us in him before the creation of the world to be holy and blameless in his sight" (Ephesians 1:4). The "in him" in this verse is referring to Christ, so Paul's point is that before time began, God wanted us to be both pure and his. But he gave us the freedom to choose him back. Being "in him" is our choice to make. We can choose God or choose to take our chances

> God chose us, and he didn't choose us after all the ones he really wanted were already spoken for. Uh-uh.

in an eternity without him. Because he loves us, he hopes we'll choose wisely. He looked across time . . . pointed at you and me . . . and said, "Those people standing there . . . in my Son, Christ . . . I'll take them." And for that, you and I should be grateful because it means that we are loved and that we are special.

God chose us, and he didn't choose us after all the ones he really wanted were already spoken for. Uh-uh. He picked us first, and that fact means something.

No. It means everything.

YOU'RE SPECIAL

The fact that God chose you first means that you're special. But before you get the big head and submit a bill to Congress setting aside the day of your birth as a national holiday, I need to point something out. If we truly understand the Bible, then we'll truly understand what it means for God to view us as special.

When we think *special,* we think birthday parties, being the line leader in elementary school, standing ovations, Christmas bonuses, a corner office, a company car, our name on a door, or our photo on a movie poster. But when God thinks *special,* he thinks of different kinds of things.

God chose Abram. He was special. God told Abram, "I will make you into a great nation and I will bless you; I will make your name great, and you will be a blessing. I will bless those who bless you, and whoever curses you I will curse; and all peoples on earth will be blessed through you" (Genesis 12:2, 3). But before God spoke those promises of things that were sure to make Abram feel special, God said, "Leave your country, your people and your father's household and go to the land I will show you" (v. 1). *What?*

God chose Moses. He was special, so God gave him the job of leading an entire nation out of bondage. God sent him to confront the most powerful ruler in the world, saying, "I am sending you to Pharaoh to bring my people the Israelites out of Egypt" (Exodus 3:10).

God chose Job . . . to be tested by Satan! "Then the Lord said to Satan, 'Have you considered my servant Job?'" (Job 1:8). Here's my paraphrase of this verse, "Then the Lord said to Satan, 'If I were you I'd pick Job first.'" God chose Job, and within twenty-one verses his family and all but one of his servants were dead and he was covered head to foot in painful sores.

God chose Jeremiah to be a prophet of God during a time when Jerusalem, the city of David, would fall to the Babylonians. God said to him, "Before I formed you in the womb I knew you, before you were born I set you apart; I appointed you as a prophet to the nations" (Jeremiah 1:5). But nine verses later, God—not wanting Jeremiah to be lulled into a false sense of security thinking that his ministry was going to be a blur of designer clothes, luxury cars, and a summer home on the coast—said, "From the north disaster will be poured out on all who live in the land" (v. 14).

God chose a young virgin named Mary to be the mother of the Lord of all mankind and then sent the angel Gabriel to tell her. (If I were Gabriel, I'd have been nervous about delivering *that* news!) Gabriel said, "Greetings, you who are highly favored! The Lord is with you" (Luke 1:28). Since Mary was a woman and women can see trouble coming from a mile away, she "wondered what kind of greeting this might be" (v. 29). Gabriel tried to console her by say-

> ## Being chosen by God is a bed of roses— with every thorn included.

ing, "Do not be afraid, Mary, you have found favor with God" (v. 30). In other words, "Mary, congratulations. You've been picked first!" Mary was going to be the mother of our Lord and be admired for all time. But before the praise, she would have to endure the stigma of being an unwed mother. And she would have to see the Son she loved be executed as a criminal. There were going to be times when Mary wasn't going to feel very special.

God incarnate chose the disciples, picking Peter and Andrew first, simply by saying, "Come, follow me . . . and I will make you fishers of men" (Matthew 4:19). They did. And they died because of their choice.

God chose me too, and life hasn't been all birthday parties, bonuses, and accolades. I can tell you from personal experience that being chosen by God is a bed of roses—with every thorn included. God has chosen many people in the past, and each of those people was tested by trials.

There will be times when we won't feel very special.

I don't feel very special right now.

It's three in the morning and I can't sleep.

My family and I are in a hotel room just south of Columbia, South Carolina, which on any other night wouldn't be a bad thing. But tonight it is. We're supposed to be home, sleeping in our own beds, in our own rooms, in our house in Kissimmee, Florida, so we'll be rested and ready for church in the morning. But the transmission in our van went out while we were driving home from vacation yesterday, so we're stuck in a hotel room, trying to figure out how we're going to get our van fixed and ourselves home.

> If God is so special to me, why don't I feel so special to him right now?

It's going to be expensive. It's already been expensive. A taxi ride, a rental van, towing expenses, a night in a hotel room, and a new transmission for my van were definitely not in the budget.

I have a headache.

I don't feel very special right now, and it doesn't really seem fair.

After all, I picked God first.

I chose him over everything else and have devoted my life to serving him. Everything in my life revolves around God. God is why I live where I live. God is the reason I attended college where I did. God is the reason I married Rhonda. God is why I don't do bad things. God is why I do good things. God is why my boys have the names they have. My faith in God is everything to me. It's why I do what I do. I've chosen to make serving God my vocation, so why am I buying a transmission at the end of my vacation?

If God is so special to me, why don't I feel so special to him right now? What's the problem?

The problem is that we human beings fell long before my transmission fell.

The problem is that we're not perfect. So this world is not perfect, and things don't always work—or work out—the way we want them to.

The problem is that we're forgetful.

No, my specific problem right now is that *I'm* forgetful.

I'm feeling frustrated because I've forgotten how much God loves me. I've forgotten the 1.2 million amazing things God has done for me. I've forgotten that he has always made something good out of something bad in my life. I've forgotten that he's never looked away from me and my family for one second. And I've forgotten that he's always provided for our needs.

I need to remember that I was picked first by God—and I need to remember that even when I feel picked *on* by God.

God chose me and he chose you, so that makes us special. And when God thinks *special,* he thinks: leaving everything, putting your son on an altar, confronting Pharaoh, boils from head to toe, Babylonians, virgin birth, mar-

> **I need to remember that I was picked first by God—and I need to remember that even when I feel picked *on* by God.**

tyrdom, and car troubles. But he also thinks: being the father of a great nation, being the liberator of millions, more blessings in the latter part of life than in the first part, being a prophet of God, being the mother of the Savior, being one of the original leaders of the church of God, being forever with God in eternity . . . and unexpected checks in the mail that cover the exact cost of transmission repairs. Which means that those who are chosen by God are special.

It also means something a little less obvious. It also means that you are needed.

YOU'RE NEEDED

Frank had a strong right leg.

Nothing got past Danny Leporatti at shortstop.

Felicity could kick the pitches that were too bouncy for the rest of us.

David was great in the outfield.

Sheila was a good pitcher.

And I was hard to hit as I ran swiftly to first base.

Each of us was picked because we filled a need, which ultimately was to play a kickball game. You can't play a kickball game without players. And you can't sail a ship to the South Pole all by yourself, so Ernest Shackleton chose a crew.

I'd have a hard time arguing with those who say that Ernest Shackleton was "the greatest leader that ever came on God's earth, bar none,"[1] but it's not for reasons they might share and you might suspect. The reason I think Shackleton was a great leader has nothing to do with achieving his goals—he failed to reach almost all of them. And it's not for leading a lot of people—he never led a group larger than twenty-seven people.

> **Every person did what he was originally chosen to do. That's why all twenty-eight men survived.**

I think Shackleton was one of the greatest leaders who ever lived because he knew how to build a good team. He was a good chooser who had an eye for talent and giftedness, and he proved that he could build a team that could survive almost anything. Each of the twenty-eight-man *Endurance* team was chosen to do a specific job. And because each man did his job well, each man on Shackleton's team survived for two years in the frozen wilderness of Antarctica when all seemed lost.

Shackleton was an explorer who was driven to reach the South Pole and explore Antarctica. So in 1902, he and two other men set out for the South Pole but failed to get within 460 miles of their goal. In 1908, Shackleton and his team tried again but had to turn back just ninety-seven miles short of the South Pole, even though three of his men had gotten closer to the geographic South Pole than anyone else.[2]

Undeterred, Shackleton again set his sights on the South Pole and began the arduous but important process of building a great team. The *Endurance* was the name of both the expedition and the ship. The mission was to be the first to cross the South Pole from sea to sea.

In 1914, Shackleton began his mission by picking his team, which was made all the more difficult because everyone wanted to join his pursuit. One historian noted, "When Shackleton announced his plans to return to the Antarctic in a letter to *The Times* in London on December 29, 1913, he was deluged with requests. Nearly five thousand hopefuls sent applications."[3] Shackleton needed only about thirty men, which he began to choose carefully because the mission was dangerous and the success of his mission depended on a good team.

Shackleton described the task of putting together an ideal team: "The men selected must be qualified for the work, and they must also have the special qualifications required to meet polar conditions. They must be able to live together in harmony for a long period of time without outside communication, and it must be remembered that the men whose desires lead them to the untrodden paths of the world have generally marked individuality. It was no easy matter for me to select the staff."[4]

One historian commenting on this mission pointed out, "There were no passengers on board the *Endurance*."[5] So when the *Endurance* became stuck in the ice on January 18, 1915 (where it stayed until eventually being crushed by the ice nine months later on November 21), and the men began a long fight for survival, every person did what he was originally chosen to do. That's why all twenty-eight men survived.

Leaders now study the life of Ernest Shackleton to learn how to survive in a crisis. They find that even though his mission failed, every man survived against impossible odds because Shackleton chose a good team and made sure that each member of that team understood his role.

God is a good chooser too.

When there is a mission and he needs a good team, he knows whom to pick first.

> # When God needed someone who could handle pain and show the rest of us what both we and Satan are capable of, he chose Job.

When God needed someone on whom to build a nation, he knew he needed someone with great faith, so he chose Abram. He knew Abram would be willing to give up his land, his name, and even his son if that's what it took to bless the world.

When God needed someone with political experience to rescue his people from bondage, tend them in a vast wilderness, and lead them to freedom, he chose Moses, a man who had grown up in Pharaoh's house and who was currently employed as a shepherd.

When God needed someone who could handle pain and show the rest of us what both we and Satan are capable of, he chose Job.

When God needed someone with courage to be a prophet to the nations, he chose Jeremiah.

When God needed someone with the strength to be a pregnant virgin, he chose Mary.

When God needed someone with passion, someone who would be willing to get out of a perfectly good boat and walk on water if that's what needed to be done, he used his first pick to choose the man that anyone else would have picked last—he chose Peter.

And when God needed someone to tell the people of this world how much he loves them, he chose you.

So look up.

Stop shuffling your feet.

Stop doubting yourself.

Stop thinking the worst.

Look at the Captain.

He's pointing at you and saying, "I choose you."

Doesn't it feel great to get picked first?

QUESTIONS ABOUT WHO YOU ARE

FOR PERSONAL STUDY AND REFLECTION: *Find a picture or item that represents a time in your life when you felt special. Reflect on the circumstances of that time before continuing with this study.*

FOR GROUP STUDY AND DISCUSSION: *Ask group members each to bring a picture or item that represents a time in their lives when they felt special. As they show their pictures or items, ask them to explain why they felt so special. Then work together to answer the questions and read the Scriptures.*

1. When they chose teams on your elementary-school playground, were you usually chosen first, in the middle, or last? How did that make you feel then? Does the memory still make you feel good/bad now?

2. Recall a time when you were selected for a special task. What did you learn about yourself as you completed the task?

3. If you were choosing (from among your acquaintances) a team to save the world, whom would you pick first? Why?

Read Genesis 12:1-4

4. Why do you think God chose Abram to be the father of the Israelites? Why do you think Abram was willing to leave everything immediately to go wherever God would lead?

5. What is one good reason Abram could have given for

not joining God's team immediately? What would have happened if Abram had not obeyed?

Read Matthew 4:18-22

---

6. Why do you think Jesus chose these men for his special mission? Why do you think they followed—immediately?

7. What is one good reason Peter, Andrew, James, and John could have given for not following Jesus immediately? What would have happened if these men had not obeyed?

Read Ephesians 1:4, 5

---

8. Why would God choose you for his special mission?

9. What reason might someone give for not following Jesus immediately?

10. What person in your life needs to know that he/she was chosen by God to be saved through Christ?

> *"Lord, thank you for choosing me to be on your team. Thank you that I can be part of something bigger than myself. I know some people who don't understand that they are chosen. This week, I am going to tell* _____
> (name of person) *that you want him/her to be on your team too. Give me wisdom, discernment, and courage as I speak."*

YOU ARE FREE

Born to fly

6

> The LORD said, "I have indeed seen the misery of my people in Egypt. I have heard them crying out because of their slave drivers, and I am concerned about their suffering. So I have come down to rescue them from the hand of the Egyptians and to bring them up . . . into a good and spacious land."
>
> EXODUS 3:7, 8

> It is for freedom that Christ has set us free. Stand firm, then, and do not let yourselves be burdened again by a yoke of slavery.
>
> GALATIANS 5:1

On May 26, 2003, an Iraqi man, Jawad Amir, experienced a long-awaited freedom. Twenty-one years before, Saddam Hussein had placed an execution order on Jawad because he supported one of Saddam's enemies. When Jawad found out about the order, he ran away, but not to a nearby town or distant country. Instead, he chose to hide in a space between two walls in his parents' home. He stayed in that tiny space for the next two decades. He was alive, but he was also imprisoned with only a peephole connecting him to the outside world.

Everyone, except for his closest family members, thought he was dead. But he was alive because of the aid of his family and a deep desire for freedom. He drank water from a nearby well and passed the time by listening to a small radio and reading the Koran, hoping that one day he would be free again.

When, in the depths of his prison between two walls, he heard that Saddam Hussein's statue in Baghdad had been pulled down, he finally decided it was safe enough to leave his hiding place. When asked how he felt, he said he was "well" and was "optimistic about the future."[1]

There's nothing like freedom to make one optimistic.

Are you free? You were created to be.

We weren't created to be comfortable in bondage or to be addicted, imprisoned, trapped, chained . . . or hidden between two walls in our parents' houses. We were born to fly.

While in college, my friend Mike worked at a central Florida theme park that displays a large number of reptiles, including alligators and crocodiles. One day, while on duty in the gift shop, Mike noticed a lot of upset people exiting the park. Mike then learned that the park officials' release of a wounded bald eagle had gone terribly wrong.

Some time before, the injured eagle had been taken into captivity to be nurtured back to health. After the eagle had lived in a cage for a long time, park officials decided it was time to release him back into the wild. But things didn't go as planned. Weakened during his captivity, the bald eagle floundered through the air until he landed in the middle of the alligator-feeding show. He was devoured within seconds, to the horror of the tourists who had gathered around the lagoon to watch alligators eat dead chickens—not live bald eagles. There was something about watching the symbol of our nation being ripped to pieces by reptiles that had the tourists running for their cars.

Bald eagles were not meant to be caged—even for their own good. They were born to fly.

> ## Bald eagles were not meant to be caged—even for their own good. They were born to fly.

So were hawks.

Another friend of mine, Terry, went to the aforementioned central Florida theme park a couple of years ago and noticed a large hawk in a cage just inside the park entrance. This bird too had been injured. But this time the park officials decided—having learned their lesson the hard way—that it would be too risky to release him. The hawk would be best kept in a big cage next to the gift shop.

Well, my friend Terry later went back to that theme park to shoot some pictures of the caged hawk for an upcoming sermon. But he found the cage sitting empty. When Terry asked the lady at the register about the hawk, she said, "It was terrible. One day he just flew into the side of the cage, broke his neck, and died."

You and Maya Angelou may know why the caged bird sings, but I know why the caged bird *dies*. The caged bird dies because birds—like us—were not designed or destined for cages. We were born to fly.

Samuel Dickey Gordon was a Boston preacher in the early 1900s. One day S. D. Gordon saw a boy carrying a beat-up, rusty birdcage containing several small, miserable birds. Curious, he asked the boy what he was going to do with the birds.

"I'm going to have some fun with them," the boy responded.

"What are you going to do after that?" Mr. Gordon asked.

"Oh, I have some cats at home, and they like birds, so I'm going to feed them to my cats," he answered.

S. D. Gordon felt sorry for the caged birds and offered to buy them.

Surprised, the boy said, "Mister, you don't want to buy these birds. They're just ugly field birds. They don't sing or anything."

Undeterred, Mr. Gordon negotiated until they had a deal.

Once he had the birdcage in his hands, he did a simple but very symbolic thing. He opened the cage, released the birds, and watched as they flew away.

> **Absolute freedom leads to absolute chaos.**

Satan wants to trap you, play with you, and then destroy you when he's through; but God has other plans for your life. God cares about you, and he cares about what happens to you.

God loves us and wants us to be free, which is why the cries of the Israelites caught the attention of the Lord. In Exodus 3:7, 8 we read: "The LORD said, 'I have indeed seen the misery of my people in Egypt. I have heard them crying out because of their slave drivers, and I am concerned about their suffering. So I have come down to rescue them from the hand of the Egyptians and to bring them up out of that land into a good and spacious land, a land flowing with milk and honey.'"

The cries of the Israelites resonated in the heart of God because God created us to be free from the very beginning.

One of the first things God said to Adam and Eve in the garden, as he was introducing them to their new home, was that they were free. God said, "You are *free* to eat from any tree in the garden" (Genesis 2:16, emphasis added). God wanted them to know that they were free, but he didn't stop there. He also needed them to know that all true freedom is not absolute freedom.

Absolute freedom leads to absolute chaos.

Imagine that all of the traffic lights, stop signs, lines on the road, speed limits, and police officers were removed from your city while you were at work today. How long do you think it would take to get home after work? Roads would be chaotic. Intersections would be clogged. Traffic would be backed up. Some people would be driving too fast, some would be driving too slowly, and some people might be too afraid to drive at all. My fifteen-minute, mostly peaceful drive home would become a treacherous and scary fight for survival.

Rules help to maintain order on our roads, in our homes, in our nation, and in this world. That's why the removal of the Ten Commandments from our legal system, the removal of moral absolutes from society, and the removal of rules and discipline in the home are all so troubling.

We are free. We were created to be free, but we were not created to be absolutely free. When God told Adam and Eve that they were "free to eat from any tree in the garden," he added, "but you must not eat from the tree of the knowledge of good and evil, for when you eat of it you will surely die" (Genesis 2:16, 17).

Boundaries are good.

Boundaries provide security by identifying areas of danger.

Divine boundaries provide identity by clarifying for us when we are, and when we are not, in a proper relationship with God. The law of Moses was the standard by which those under the old covenant knew whether they were OK with God, and a relationship with Jesus is the standard by which those under the new covenant do the same.

After liberating the Israelites from their Egyptian bondage, one of the first things the Lord did was to lay down the law (Exodus 20), and God reiterated the law of Moses forty years later as the Israelites were preparing to enter the promised land (Deuteronomy 5). Freedom from bondage in Egypt into absolute freedom without any rules in the wilderness would have led to bondage of a more barbaric sort, as the strong would have made the rules, and the weak would have been enslaved again.

God wanted the children of Israel to be free, so he liberated them.

God wanted the children of Israel to be *truly* free, so he gave them the law to govern their freedom. But that was only a temporary solution to our eternal problem. That's why God—wanting us to be truly free for all time—sent Jesus, at just the right time.

As Jesus began his ministry, he went to the synagogue in Nazareth and made one thing perfectly clear to the people in his hometown: "The Spirit of the Lord is on me, because he has anointed me to preach good news to the poor. He has sent me to proclaim *freedom* for the prisoners and recovery of sight for the blind, to release the oppressed, to proclaim the year of the Lord's favor" (Luke 4:18, 19, emphasis added).

This is great news! Jesus has heard our cries and has come to set us free.

If you are in bondage to pornography . . . he knows, and he's come to set you free.

> God—wanting us to be truly free for all time—sent Jesus, at just the right time.

If you are in bondage to alcohol . . . he knows, and he's come to set you free.

If you are in bondage to depression . . . he knows, and he's come to set you free.

If you are in bondage to prescription drugs . . . he knows, and he's come to set you free.

If you are in bondage to anger . . . he knows, and he's come to set you free.

If you are in bondage to gambling . . . he knows, and he's come to set you free.

If you are in bondage to same-sex attraction . . . he knows, and he's come to set you free.

If you are in bondage to an eating disorder . . . he knows, and he's come to set you free.

If you are in bondage to debt . . . he knows, and he's come to set you free.

If you are in bondage to these or any other oppressors . . . he knows, and he's come to set you free.

And he knows that without his help, all of us are in bondage to death. He knows, and he's come to set us free.

God wants you to believe and accept this.

He asks you to step out of your shackles and embrace the truth that "if the Son sets you free, you will be free indeed" (John 8:36) and "where the Spirit of the Lord is, there is freedom" (2 Corinthians 3:17).

When we have a relationship with Christ, we are free. But remember that although this freedom is absolutely real, eternal, and wonderful, this freedom is not absolute.

FREE *FROM* SIN BUT NOT FREE *TO* SIN

The children of Israel learned this lesson the hard way.

God had been clear: "You shall not make for yourself an idol in the form of anything in heaven above or on the earth beneath or in the waters below. You shall not bow down to them or worship them; for I, the LORD your God, am a jealous God, punishing the children for the sin of the fathers to the third and fourth generation of those who hate me, but showing love to a thousand generations of those who love me and keep my commandments" (Exodus 20:4-6). But the Israelites made a golden idol and worshiped it. So the Lord responded, and three thousand people were executed (Exodus 32:28).

God had been clear: "You shall have no other gods before me" (Exodus 20:3). But the Israelite men committed sexual immorality with the Moabite women and worshiped their god, Baal, so the Lord struck down twenty-four thousand of them with a plague (Numbers 25:9).

God had been clear: "If you obey me fully and keep my covenant, then out of all nations you will be my treasured possession" (Exodus 19:5). And the Israelites had been clear in responding to these rules ("obey me" and "keep my covenant") when they answered together, "We will do everything the LORD has said" (v. 8). Then the Israelites sinned by continually doing evil in the wilderness, and God banished all but Joshua and Caleb from entering the promised land. God said, "'Because they have not followed me wholeheartedly, not one of the men twenty years old or more who came up out of Egypt will see the land I promised on oath to Abraham, Isaac and Jacob—not one except Caleb son of Jephunneh the Kenizzite and Joshua son of Nun, for they followed the LORD wholeheartedly.' The LORD's anger burned against Israel and he made them wander in the desert forty years, until the whole generation of those who had done evil in his sight was gone" (Numbers 32:11-13).

> "They followed the LORD wholeheartedly."

Although we on this side of the cross are free, being no longer under the law but under a system of grace, God still expects us to avoid sin. To the Christians in Galatia Paul wrote, "You, my brothers, were called to be free. But do not use your freedom to indulge the sinful nature" (Galatians 5:13).

That kind of freedom can be deadly.

I had a lovely friend named Hannah. She had a beautiful face, a beautiful voice, and a soul to match. Hannah was a good person, blessed with the ability to connect with the outcasts in our high school. I knew her well. She and I performed a scene together from the Broadway musical *Bye, Bye, Birdie*; and even now as I think about how well she looked and played her part, her memory makes me smile. She was a dear friend, but I'm talking about her in past tense because she's dead.

She used the newfound freedom of college to make some poor choices. During the first semester of her first year of college, Hannah got into partying. One night after drinking too much, Hannah climbed out the window of her third-floor dorm room. She was on her way to her boyfriend's room after curfew, but she never made it. She slipped off the ledge and fell three floors to her death.

Satan is our Pharaoh, our Saddam, our enemy. He wants to put us in a cage next to the gift shop until we break our necks—or our spirits—

on the side of the cage in a desperate attempt to free ourselves. Satan wants us trapped within the walls of our homes, believing that he's in charge of the outside world and that escape is futile. Satan wants to take us home and feed us to his cats. Satan will try to lure us onto the ledge with the temptation of more pleasure, more fun, and more freedom; but even though we have the freedom to climb out the window, we must not. Satan is a slave master intent on filling the dungeons of Hell with the souls of those who used their freedom to eat from the wrong tree.

But just as sure as Satan is a slave master—intent on our eternal bondage, Jesus is the master of slaves—intent on our eternal liberation.

FREE TO SERVE

The moment Christ freed me from my sin, I became his slave. To the church in Corinth Paul wrote, "He who was a slave when he was called by the Lord is the Lord's freedman; similarly, he who was a free man when he was called is Christ's slave" (1 Corinthians 7:22).

And not only am I *Christ's* slave, I am also yours.

I'm a pretty good server. I paid my way through college and graduate school by working as a waiter. I loved the job. It was an opportunity to meet people and make quick money. I was good at it and was always one of the top five servers at my restaurant, so I was eventually given the responsibility of training new servers.

I loved the people. I enjoyed giving customers a memorable and pleasant experience, and I wanted them to be so pleased that they would ask for me the next time they came in. I prided myself on meeting my guests' every need and exceeding their expectations.

Yes, I'm a pretty good server, but I'm a pretty bad servant.

I don't always like the job. Preaching is fun, but it's all the other stuff that can be so annoying. I know that Jesus washed his disciples' feet, and I know that foot washing was a pretty disgusting job. But I think I would rather wash your feet and scrub your toes than have to sit next to you in a board meeting or go visit your house after I've found out you're upset with me. I'd rather wash your feet than try to keep you from leaving the church because another member hurt your feelings. Not to mention listening to your complaints about the volume of the music we sang last Sunday. But because I do love my job and I desperately love the people I serve, I have no choice. If I want to be truly free in Christ, I have to serve you. When Christ liberated me, he enslaved me to you for benefit on both sides.

> "You, my brothers, were called to be free."

Paul points this out in the part of Galatians 5:13 that I left out earlier. Let's look at the entire verse this time. Paul wrote, "You, my brothers, were called to be free. But do not use your freedom to indulge the sinful nature; *rather, serve one another in love.*" (emphasis added)

I am also more than Christ's slave and your slave. I am—for the sake of the gospel—everyone's slave. Paul wrote, "Though I am free and belong to no man, I make myself a slave to everyone, to win as many as possible" (1 Corinthians 9:19). True freedom can be truly realized only by becoming a servant of Christ and of all people.

Serving Christ and all people will liberate us.

Serving Christ and all people will liberate others.

One day a prairie chicken found an egg and sat on it until it hatched. Unbeknownst to the prairie chicken, inside the egg was an eagle. While the eagle is the greatest of all birds, soaring above the heights with grace and ease, the prairie chicken doesn't even know how to fly. Predictably, the little eagle, being raised in a family of prairie chickens, thought he was a prairie chicken. He walked around, ate garbage, and clucked like a prairie chicken. One day he looked up to see a majestic bald eagle soaring through the air. He asked his family what it was. They responded, "It's an eagle. But you could never be like that because you are just a prairie chicken." Then they returned to pecking the garbage. The eagle spent his whole life looking up at eagles, longing to join them among the clouds. It never once occurred to him to lift his wings and try to fly. The eagle died thinking he was a prairie chicken, never realizing he was born to fly.

You and I were not created to live in bondage in Egypt.

You and I were not created to live our lives in a chicken pen.

You and I were not created to eat garbage off the ground.

No! This ground is not our home; the sky is our destiny. We were created to be free. We were born to fly!

QUESTIONS ABOUT WHO YOU ARE

FOR PERSONAL STUDY AND REFLECTION: *Lock yourself in a quiet room for this time of study and reflection. Afterwards, unlock the door and fly away through the rest of the day!*

FOR GROUP STUDY AND DISCUSSION: *Place an empty birdcage in the center of the room. At some time during the group study (perhaps after question 6 or 10), ask each person to list on a separate piece of paper the things that Satan is trying to use to enslave them. At the end of the study time, have prayer and ask members to tear up their lists and place the pieces inside the cage. You will discard these later.*

1. What's the first image that pops into your mind when you hear the word *freedom*?

2. Recall a moment in your life when you felt the most free. Is that moment a distant memory or a present reality?

3. Has there ever been a time in your life when you felt enslaved? Why?

Read Exodus 3:7, 8

---

4. Have you ever been rescued from something? If so, how did you get into a situation from which you had to be rescued? Who was your hero, and how were you rescued?

5. What kinds of things are people enslaved to?

Read Galatians 5:1

6. What are the top three things that consume most of your time in a typical week? Do those things make you feel more liberated or more enslaved?

7. Paul reminds us that "it is for freedom that Christ has set us free." What is one thing you can do to make freedom more of a focus in the next week?

Read Acts 16:16-36

8. Why were Paul and Silas imprisoned?

9. What was their response to being placed in jail? What was God's response? What was the jailer's response to God's response?

10. What is going to be your response now that you know you were born to fly?

   "Lord, I realize that you're in the business of setting people free. Thank you for liberating me from _____

   (specific problem or situation). *I know that I was born to fly. Help me to know you even better so I can soar for your glory every day of my life."*

YOU ARE LOVED

His "mine"

In your unfailing love you will lead the people you have redeemed.

EXODUS 15:13

I will sing of the LORD's great love forever.

PSALM 89:1

For God so loved the world that he gave his one and only Son, that whoever believes in him shall not perish but have eternal life.

JOHN 3:16

I wish I could find a way to express to you how much God loves you.

I love everything about love. I love falling in love. I love thinking about love. I love listening to music about love. I love writing about love, and I love being in love.

The first time I remember being in love was when I was five years old. Now, I loved my parents, grandparents, and my three sibli— Well . . . I loved my parents and grandparents. But I never really was "in love" until one spring day at a church campout near Hamilton, Ohio.

Her name was Lynette, the location was the campground outhouse called the Silver Bullet, and the event was my first kiss. Though we didn't know what we were doing—or what we were smelling—it didn't stop us from sharing a first kiss and kindling a first love.

But that didn't last.

The next time I remember being in love was in the fourth grade. Her name was Sheila, the location was Audubon Park Elementary—Room 5, and the event was Valentine's Day. Valentine's Day was a big deal when I was a kid. Each student prepared for the big day by stapling two sides of a file folder and then decorating it with hearts, cupids, and the like. We then taped our Valentine's Day folders to the corners of our desks. The night before Valentine's Day, my mom would go to the drugstore and get a bag of small valentines, the kind that had a place for the recipient's name, a place for the sender's name, and a generic message that said something like "Be Mine" or "True Love" or the always safe "Happy Valentine's Day!"

Anyway, I was deeply in love with Sheila, and I decided it was time to let her know how much I loved her. So after filling out valentines for Felicity, Mary Catherine, Wendy, that girl who picked her nose, and my friend Frank, I prepared to fill out Sheila's valentine.

I put on some Barry Manilow music, lit some candles, set my favorite picture of Sheila (that just also happened to include everyone else from my fourth grade class, since it was a class picture) on the corner of my desk, bowed my head, and asked for God's blessing on this important step of faith. I then carefully filled out Sheila's valentine. To: Sheila Wagner. From: Arron Chambers. Message: Happy Valentine's Day! Love, Arron.

The next day as Sheila read my valentine and the word *love* that signified that this was no ordinary valentine, she smiled; and our relationship began. We were "going out"—as much as two fourth-grade kids can "go out" when their parents don't know about it, they can't drive, and the entire relationship has to take place during lunch and on the playground during recess.

But that didn't last.

And neither did any of the other times I fell in love during elementary, junior high, and high school, until . . . at college I met a cute

> ## I made her change her name and promise before God that she'd love me until the day I stop breathing.

little redhead from Tennessee named Rhonda and finally knew what it meant to be in love. I made her change her name and promise before God that she'd love me until the day I stop breathing.

Now, sixteen years and four kids later, I'm just beginning to understand what true love really feels like.

I wish I could go back in time and speak to myself at age eighteen.

If I could I'd say, "Arron, don't be an idiot!"

And, "I know you are going to think it's a good idea to dump Rhonda—even though she's the girl you've always dreamed of—so you aren't 'tied down' during summer break. But if you do, you're going to miss almost two years of being with her. Don't be stupid!"

I might also tell myself, "You keep telling her that you love her, but you only think you know what that word means. Trust me. I am—I mean, *we* are—thirty-seven years old now and just starting to understand what the word *love* really means. If God blesses this marriage with . . . say, eighty years, you'll only then be close to understanding what the word *love* really means. Oh, and one more thing . . . You're going to be tempted to set the alarm on your watch and put it in the overhead projector in your English comp class next semester. Trust me, it's not as funny as you think it is, and it's not going to end well."

I wish I could find a way to express to you how much I love Rhonda and how much more amazing love is after sixteen years of marriage.

Love like this is transformational. My wife's love has changed my life.

Love like this is powerful. I would die for my wife.

Love like this is sustaining. I don't know how I could survive one minute without my wife's love.

Love like this is also imperfect. As committed as we both are to our wedding vows, my wife and I live as sinners in a fallen world. We have seen faithful love ruined by unfaithfulness, so we know that the love in our relationship is vulnerable to sin and must be nourished and protected. Our love is strong. Our love is pure. But we both also know that—

> There is no guarantee that we will always love each other the way we do right now.

because we are not God—our love is imperfect. There is no guarantee that we will always love each other the way we do right now. Our love, as incredible as it is, doesn't come close to God's love. We are fickle, but God is faithful.

I wish I could find a way to express to you how much God loves you.

His love for us—unlike human love—is unfailing.

GOD'S UNFAILING LOVE

The Hebrew word for *unfailing love* (*hesed*)[1] is used more than any other word in the Bible to describe God's love for us.

It's the word Moses and the Israelites sang to describe the kind of love that helped them escape Pharaoh's army and cross the Red Sea: "In your unfailing love you will lead the people you have redeemed. In your strength you will guide them to your holy dwelling" (Exodus 15:13).

It's the word Moses used to describe the kind of love that can truly satisfy, when he prayed, "Satisfy us in the morning with your unfailing love, that we may sing for joy and be glad all our days" (Psalm 90:14).

It's the word an unknown psalmist used to describe the kind of love that remained faithful to the Israelites, even though *they* did not. He repeated four times, "Let them give thanks to the LORD for his unfailing love" (Psalm 107:8, 15, 21, 31).

It's the word used by Jewish worshipers—twenty-six times—to describe the kind of love that is praiseworthy. With thankful hearts they repeatedly testified, "His love endures forever" (Psalm 136).

It's the word David used to describe the love that would keep him from drowning in a sea of guilt. David pleaded, "Turn, O LORD, and deliver me; save me because of your unfailing love" (Psalm 6:4).

It's the word David used to describe the kind of love that saved him. David sang, "I trust in your unfailing love; my heart rejoices in your salvation" (Psalm 13:5).

It's the word David used to describe the love that protected him. "How priceless is your unfailing love! Both high and low among men find refuge in the shadow of your wings" (Psalm 36:7).

It's the word David used to describe the love that made him want to sing. "I will praise you, O LORD, among the nations; I will sing of you among the peoples. For great is your love, higher than the heavens; your faithfulness reaches to the skies" (Psalm 108:3, 4).

Based on the number of times David used the word *hesed,* it appears that he may have been more appreciative of God's unfailing love than all other writers in the Bible. Maybe that's because he knew *failing* love more than the others did.

David was a man chosen by God to be the king of his people (1 Samuel 16), a man whom the prophet Samuel and Luke said was "a man after [God's] own heart" (1 Samuel 13:14; Acts 13:22). He was also a man who saw a woman named Bathsheba taking a bath and, overcome with lust, slept with her and then sent her husband to the front line of battle to be killed.

David failed the Lord, but the love of the Lord never failed David. So *hesed* is the word David used after being confronted with his sins to describe the love that he needed if he was to have any hope. In repentance David proclaimed, "Have mercy on me, O God, according to your unfailing love; according to your great compassion blot out my transgressions" (Psalm 51:1).

> ## Have you ever taken off your wedding ring while leaving for a business trip?

Has your love ever failed?

Have you walked out when you should have stayed?

Have you ever missed one of your son's soccer games after promising you wouldn't?

Have you ever spoken a harsh word when you should have remained silent?

Have you ever forgotten your anniversary?

Have you ever smiled at the news of an enemy's suffering?

Have you ever hired a divorce attorney?

Have you ever taken off your wedding ring while leaving for a business trip?

Have you ever imagined yourself making love with someone other than your spouse?

Have you ever broken a friend's confidence?

Have you ever been unkind to your parents . . . or dumped the girl of your dreams?

God wouldn't do any of those things.

His love for us is unfailing.

GOD'S INCOMPREHENSIBLE LOVE

I wish I could find a way to express to you how much God loves you.

Let me give it a shot.

My great-uncle Vernon "Vernie" Miller was a very successful businessman. He was also a man of God who loved his wife, Norma, unfailingly. When Aunt Norma was diagnosed with Alzheimer's, Uncle Vernie devoted himself to caring for her. He sold everything that didn't matter and invested in only what did. He purchased an RV, and he and Aunt Norma spent the next decade visiting family, friends, and ministries they supported. Uncle Vernie wanted to keep Aunt Norma's mind—and heart—stimulated, so he surrounded her with love and loved ones.

During this period of time, Uncle Vernie and Aunt Norma visited our home several times. Each time they came to our house during those years, we noticed that Aunt Norma was drifting further and further away, like a helium balloon that slips out of your fingers at the fair and drifts slowly into the sky—and there's absolutely nothing you can do but watch as it floats beyond the reach of your outstretched arms.

Uncle Vernie's love for Aunt Norma was amazing. During their last visit, Uncle Vernie—with a smile on his face—lovingly fed, cleaned, wiped, spoke to, spoke for, and held the hand of the girl of his dreams.

She died in the spring with Uncle Vernie at her side.

Uncle Vernie's love for Aunt Norma reminds me of God's love for you.

I wish I could find another way to express how much God loves you.

Last summer, something miraculous happened in east Tennessee. I had been speaking at a conference in Missouri and was on my way to meet my wife and kids in Kentucky, so I wasn't with my family when they took my in-laws out to dinner at one of Johnson City, Tennessee's finest restaurants, the House of Ribs. (It's our tradition to take my wife's parents out to eat on the last night of every visit with them.)

After dinner, Rhonda, the kids, and her parents went home and were preparing for bed when they realized that they had left our three-year-old son's blanket at the House of Ribs. He called the blanket "mine."

Sylas was inconsolable. The worn blanket may have looked like a deteriorating ball of string to you, but to Sylas it was everything. They immediately called the restaurant, but it was already closed for the night. Rhonda was heartbroken as Sylas cried himself to sleep.

Rhonda and the kids had to leave early the next morning to meet up with me, so my mother-in-law agreed to call the restaurant about Sylas's blanket. She finally got through about 11:00 AM. The kind woman on the other end remembered seeing the blanket but recalled that they thought it was just an old rag, so they had thrown it away. The Nice House of Ribs Lady said that she would check the trash and call back.

The Nice House of Ribs Lady, her coworker, and the Christlike Man on a Smoke Break dug through that dumpster looking for my son's blanket.

One hour later the Nice House of Ribs Lady did call back with "some good news and some bad news." The good news was they had found Sylas's "mine," but the bad news was where they found it.

The Nice House of Ribs Lady had checked all of the trash cans, but they had already been emptied. So she extended Sylas an extraordinary grace by not giving up on his "mine." She and another coworker had climbed into the dumpster behind the restaurant to search. As they searched, a man on a smoke break from an adjoining business noticed these two in the dumpster and asked what they were doing.

"A three-year-old boy lost his blanket last night, and we think it's in here."

You won't believe what happened next!

The Christlike Man on a Smoke Break said, "My four-year-old has a blanket. Let me help." So the Nice House of Ribs Lady, her coworker, and the Christlike Man on a Smoke Break dug through that dumpster looking for my son's blanket.

They found it in the bottom of a plastic bag in the bottom of the dumpster, covered in coffee grounds, lettuce, and scraps of prime rib. They rescued it, and my mother-in-law drove over to pick it up.

The love that Sylas had for his blanket and the love that would place three people in a dumpster, digging through trash to look for the blanket of a stranger's son, reminds me of God's love for you.

I wish I could find another way to express how much God loves you.

There was a tree in a garden a long time ago. God told a man and a woman not to eat any fruit from that tree. The man and woman disobeyed God, and men and women have been disobeying God ever since. But God has never stopped loving us.

We continually choose sin, knowing it breaks God's heart, and he continually chooses to love us.

We had no hope of salvation. We were lost and destined for the dumpster of eternal death. But God loved us; that's why he decided to give us another chance. He sent his Son, Jesus, to this world so that all people could know that they are loved.

John—"the disciple whom Jesus loved" (John 21:20)—records it this way: "For God so loved the world that he gave his one and only Son, that whoever believes in him shall not perish but have eternal life" (John 3:16).

It's difficult to express completely how much God loves you.

He loves you so much that he will never leave your side. If you got Alzheimer's, he would sell everything he owned and spend the rest of your life helping you make memories with your loved ones before the memories of your loved ones drifted from your mind.

He loves you so much that he would crawl through a dumpster to get you back—though some people might not think you're worth the bother. You're his "mine," and he'd cry himself to sleep each night if you weren't in his arms.

We can't possibly comprehend his unfailing love . . . but we *can* accept it!

QUESTIONS ABOUT WHO YOU ARE

FOR PERSONAL STUDY AND REFLECTION: *For this time of deeper study and reflection, you'll need paper and an envelope. And you'll need something (can, jar, box, etc.) to use as a time capsule.*

FOR GROUP STUDY AND DISCUSSION: *Ask group members to bring something they love to the meeting. Begin this study by asking group members to explain why they love their items. Then move into the questions and Scriptures. For questions 7 and 8, provide paper and an envelope for each group member, as well as one item to use as a time capsule (can, jar, box, etc.). Let members share and discuss some things from their lists. Decide ahead of time where you will bury the group's time capsule.*

1. When was the first time you remember saying the words *I love you*?

2. When was the first time you remember *hearing* the words *I love you*?

3. What was the name of your first love? How did you meet him or her?

4. During what period of your life have you felt the most loved? Why?

Read Psalm 136

---

5. Count how many times in that passage the psalmist says, "His love endures forever." Do you think that covers it?

Read Psalm 89:1

---

6. What is the most significant way God has expressed his love to you?

7. This psalm was written by Ethan the Ezrahite. He says that with his "mouth [he] will make [God's] faithfulness known through all generations." On a separate sheet of paper, list some of the ways God has been faithful to you. Spend some time reflecting on the list.

8. Sign your list, date it, and seal it in the envelope. Place the envelope in your time capsule. After a time of prayer, bury the capsule in a safe and secure location.

"Lord, I have sometimes forgotten or been unaware of your unfailing love. But I know you have stuck by me in many ways. I have testified to that on my list. I pray that this written testimony can be used to share your faithfulness with future generations. Help me to testify of your love verbally this week."

YOU ARE A SAINT
The stinky house 8

> The foundations of the earth are the LORD's; upon
> them he has set the world. He will guard the feet of
> his saints, but the wicked will be silenced in darkness.
>
> 1 SAMUEL 2:8, 9

> I pray that you, being rooted and established in
> love, may have power, together with all the saints,
> to grasp how wide and long and high and deep
> is the love of Christ, and to know this love that
> surpasses knowledge—that you may be filled to
> the measure of all the fullness of God.
>
> EPHESIANS 3:17-19

When the Sunday school teacher asked her fourth-grade class, "What is a saint?" Travis's mind drifted back to Europe.

This question made my mind drift too. I was curious about the kind of information that might be out there explaining what it takes to become a saint. So I Googled "How does someone become a saint?" What I found was the Roman Catholic explanation. The process by which the Catholic Church identifies someone as a saint is called canonization. The Catholic Church has canonized more than three thousand people. People used to become saints through public opinion, but in the tenth century, Pope John XV decided that it might be wise to develop a process for identifying someone as a saint. Canonization has been revised over the years into the current system for deciding whom God has identified as saints. Here's how one becomes a Roman Catholic saint, according to the HowStuffWorks Web site:

1. A local bishop investigates the candidate's life and writings for evidence of heroic virtue. The information uncovered by the bishop is sent to the Vatican.

2. A panel of theologians and the cardinals of the Congregation for Cause of Saints evaluates the candidate's life.

3. If the panel approves, the pope proclaims that the candidate is venerable, which means that the person is a role model of Catholic virtues.

4. The next step toward sainthood is beatification. Beatification allows a person to be honored by a particular group or region. In order to beatify a candidate, it must be shown that the person is responsible for a posthumous miracle. Martyrs, those who died for their religious cause, can be beatified without evidence of a miracle. . . .

5. In order for the candidate to be considered a saint, there must be proof of a second posthumous miracle. If there is, the person is canonized.[1]

Then I began to wonder, *How many Catholic saints are there?* I Googled that question and found that "there are over 10,000 named saints . . . but no definitive 'head count.'"[2]

As a minister, I've been fairly comfortable with my definition of *saint*. But reading about the requirements of miracles and martyrdom and seeing that number of ten thousand gave me second thoughts. I know a lot of great Christians—maybe thousands—and I know that there have been a number of great Christians since the time of Christ whom I don't know. And if Christ doesn't come back during my lifetime, there are going to be still more Christians that I'll never know. If there ever is a "head count," I don't want me (or anyone) to be missed.

I've pictured myself as one of the group "when the saints go marching in" to Heaven.

I've pictured myself as one of the group "when the saints go marching in" to Heaven. So I became a little concerned. Am I really a saint . . . or am I just a delusional sinner?

What is a saint?

I've had older ladies ask me for help, saying, "Would you be a saint and bring me the book sitting on that table over there?"

Would I be a saint? Yes, I'd love to be one! But this seems to be the other extreme. Is nothing more involved in sainthood than running an errand for an elderly lady?

So I decided to revisit the Bible's definition of a saint. I know that the name *saint* is important because we, believers, are called saints sixty-nine times in the Bible. Interestingly, we are called Christians only one time (Acts 11:26).

What is a saint?

Travis's mind drifted back to a cathedral he and his family had visited in southern France. He could still hear the whispers of visitors whose speech had been quieted by a sense of the majesty of God. Travis could still feel the atmosphere of a room in which so much of importance had happened. He could yet smell the overwhelming fragrance of old wood, books, dust, and stone. And Travis, still remembering being overwhelmed by the sight of multicolored sunbeams jutting through the faces of the people immortalized in stained glass around the cathedral, answered, "A saint is someone the light shines through."

OK, I've heard this story told by ministers on several occasions, and I always find myself distracted by my opinion that Travis seems a little precocious for a kid in a fourth-grade Sunday school class. The stained glass definition is cute, but—in my opinion—cute doesn't really cut it these days.

If you had asked me "What is a saint?" when I was in fourth grade, I would have said that a saint is a guy on a pro football team from New Orleans that doesn't win very many games.

> **You and I—in Christ—have been set apart for a sacred purpose.**

The truth is that anyone who is in Christ is a saint. A saint is not fragile like a stained glass window. A saint is not a sweet senior citizen's servant boy or an average football player on a below-average team. And a saint is not defined by working miracles or being martyred.

All followers of Christ are saints. In the Bible the word used for *saint* means "consecrated to God."[3] In other words, you and I—in Christ— have been set apart for a sacred purpose.

A PEDESTAL

I can *do* set apart from the world.

I'm sitting in a comfortable chair at a coffee shop inside my favorite bookstore. I come here to drink a twenty-ounce vanilla crème frappe, listen to Norah Jones, and write stuff about Jesus. This is my place. I've been here every day this week, happily sitting next to my favorite end table. But I was a little annoyed when I arrived a few minutes ago.

There was a transient-looking guy, who smelled like dirty socks, sitting in the chair next to mine. He really stank. He was snoring when I arrived. Then he woke up, and then he was talking. Loudly. He was rambling to no one, and everyone, about how badly people drive in this town. And he connected that with a phrase, over and over again, about "some guy and Moby Dick." But from what he was saying, I'm pretty sure he's never read the book, because *Moby Dick* had nothing to do with cars.

Honestly, I was annoyed before I even sat down. And I was annoyed after situating myself next to him. I was happy when he wandered off a couple of minutes ago.

As he walked away and I began to smile, I stopped smiling when I realized that I'm a big hypocrite.

I stink.

Here I am writing about being a saint, but here I am also acting like a big jerk and not acting like Jesus.

Jesus, with unfailing love, would have talked to that man, asked where he was from, asked about his family, and offered to buy him a twenty-ounce vanilla crème frappe.

We aren't given the luxury of being saints isolated in our private little worlds without sinners—not just because it's impossible (we're all sinners, saints included) but also because it's disobedient. God commanded *all* saints to take his love to *all* people everywhere (Matthew 28:19, 20) . . . even if it's in your favorite bookstore coffee shop.

Being a saint does not give us permission to set ourselves apart from the people of this world.

David Blaine is an amazing illusionist, but I find him a little odd.

He's the guy who buried himself alive under a sidewalk in New York City back in 1999 and in an ice cube the next year.

A few years ago Blaine did something that caught my attention—not because it was amazing, but because it was first done by a "saint." In 2002, David Blaine spent thirty-five hours on top of a ninety-foot pole. He got the idea for the stunt from a man known as Saint Simeon the Stylite.

Simeon was a monk who lived as a hermit in the early 400s.[4] He did some pretty amazing things after he became a monk, like memorizing the book of Psalms. He didn't do some pretty normal things, like living on the ground!

In the year 423, Simeon answered what he considered to be a call from the Lord to live on a ten-foot-high pillar. He did that for four years, until he felt the Lord's call to start living on a sixty-five-foot-high pole, which he did for the remaining thirty years of his life. Nothing could bring Simeon down from his perch. At night he chained himself to the pole to make sure that he didn't fall to the ground.

From his tower high above the ground, Simeon would preach to the people below twice a day, offer prayers, and answer letters he received from all around the world. Simeon was revered throughout the Christian world, inspiring other monks to follow his example. His disciples, the Stylites, followed his example by mounting their own poles, but were never as famous as Simeon.

Simeon lived on a pole for more than thirty years to be holy and live above the world. And for this he's considered a saint?

A real saint is a Christian who lives a life set apart from the world. But that life is still lived *in* the world, not above it.

The saints to whom the apostle Paul wrote lived *in* the world, in cities like Rome (Romans 1:7), Jerusalem (Romans 15:25), Corinth (1 Corinthians 6:2), Ephesus (Ephesians 1:1), Philippi (Philippians 1:1) . . .

Paul says that there were even saints living in Caesar's household (Philippians 4:22). How could that be? Didn't these saints know the kind of man Caesar was? All emperors were called Caesar, but we know that this Roman emperor's name was really Nero, and we know from history that Nero was a really bad man who invented new ways to persecute Christians. How could the saints risk tainting themselves by remaining in his household? Well, these particular saints probably had no choice. Some of these saints may have been relatives, but others were certainly members of Nero's court who couldn't leave because they were legally required to serve Nero.

But we can see from the Bible that true saints are spiritually required to remain in this world. Jesus teaches that we are "the light of the world. A city on a hill cannot be hidden" (Matthew 5:14). This world needs light, and that light must be accessible, not on a platform sixty-five feet above the ground and not hidden behind stained glass windows on the corner of Main Street.

We can't *do* set apart from the world.

> **Being a saint means that we are set apart—not *from* the world—but *for* God.**

We must be a part of this world if the people of this world are to have any hope of salvation and any part of eternity. This is why, on the last night of his life, Jesus prayed, "My prayer is not that you take them out of the world but that you protect them from the evil one" (John 17:15).

Being a saint means that we are set apart—not *from* the world—but *for* God.

A LIVING ROOM

My in-laws remodeled their house a few years ago. They have a nice but modest home, and they have a nice but growing family. So they decided to knock down the wall between the family/kitchen room and the living room.

The living room was a nice room, but it was also the room in the house where all the valuable furniture, artwork, and heirlooms were kept. It had been set apart from the rest of the house as a kind of sacred place, the room for all the nice stuff.

My visits in that room felt like visits to a local museum, with black-and-white pictures of people who looked like my wife and kids, an antique piano, lacy pillows on nice but rarely used furniture, and—for some unknown reason—a lava lamp.

That room had also been set apart for a sacred purpose: Christmas.

It was the room where we gathered to open our Christmas presents. It didn't matter that the living room was one of the smallest rooms in the house; it was our tradition. So we gathered, ripped open our presents quickly, and got out of there as fast as we could, lest we become the next exhibit destined to spend eternity sitting on a doily next to the lava lamp.

> That room had also been set apart for a sacred purpose: Christmas.

Everything changed when my in-laws knocked down the wall between the family room and the living room. It was amazing! The house seemed so much bigger, and the family room and living room became one big room in which we could actually live. My in-laws got rid of the old furniture, moved the older pictures to other locations in the house, and put the lava lamp in the back bedroom where my wife and I sleep when we visit. Thanks.

The new living room is the hub of life in that home. It's functional. It's enjoyable. It's where we live.

And that's my point.

If you belong to Jesus, you are a saint, one who has been set apart to God for a special purpose. But that purpose is not to become an old room full of memories and artifacts that is visited by the living only on occasion.

We must not allow our spiritual lives to begin to mirror what we do with some of our church buildings. Sometimes, in pursuit of so-called consecration, we have turned our church buildings into dusty museums full of old pictures of who we used to be and of what we used to do. The furniture is clean but old and uncomfortable. In remote corners of the building, you'll find a few kind inhabitants who speak only about "the good ol' days," say "back in my day" a lot, and who smell a little like mothballs.

No, we are saints, set apart by God to be full of life.

He wants to live in us and through us.

He doesn't want to visit us just at Christmastime. He wants to delight in us every day of every year.

A STINKY HOUSE

A few years ago, just before the birth of our fourth child, my wife and I decided to see whether there were any bigger houses in our community that were also within our price range. We had a nice but modest home, which was feeling very full. We asked a couple in our church who are realtors to keep their eyes open for something that could provide us room to grow.

One day Cristina called to say she had something we needed to look at. She warned us that this house had been foreclosed on and was in bad shape but was worth seeing.

Our kids were with us when the door opened, and we were all horrified.

Immediately, the two oldest kids yelled, "This house stinks!"

It did.

It was horrible. We were sure that we were going to find a dead animal in one of the rooms. The previous owners had obviously left in a hurry, because the house was a disaster with empty wine bottles in the living room, clothes on the stairs, moldy food . . .

The carpet was severely soiled, the pantry was black with mold, the walls were splattered with . . . I don't even know *what* the walls were splattered with, but it was nasty. The ceiling had large, yellow water stains from an upstairs leak that had been ignored.

The house had a pool, which looked like a dark green pond.

Shrimplike creatures were swimming in it. Photos of this pool showed ducks floating around. How did ducks get into a pool enclosed by screens? Now, though, only a few of the screens were in place, and most of those were torn.

The house was a smelly disaster, but my wife and I saw potential.

A beautiful community park and playground were nearby. There was also a real lake behind the house that looked like a nice place to fish. My wife and I realized that this was not only a good deal, it was going to be a great place to raise our kids.

> A saint is simply a "stinky house" that is no longer a stinky house.

We bought what we all called the Stinky House and moved in. The restoration began. The carpet was removed and replaced. The floors, walls, and ceiling were all cleaned and repainted. My friend Marvin and I cleaned the pool, replaced the filter and the screens . . . and the pool turned blue.

Friends and family joined in, and before long the Stinky House was no more. It was now the Chambers House. When we moved in, everything changed. Even the purpose of the house changed from being simply a residence to being a residence that belonged to God and was a tool for reaching people for Christ.

Our small group from church began meeting in our house, and within two months I had the privilege of baptizing the fiancé of one of the ladies in our small group. Derek was just the first of many people who have been baptized in our pool.

What is a saint?

Remember, a saint doesn't have to be isolated or martyred—and there's not a limited number of them. They don't have to work miracles either.

A saint is simply a "stinky house" that is no longer a stinky house, because someone moved in, remodeled, redecorated, and re-created everything that was broken so that it doesn't stink anymore.

Oh . . . the transient-looking guy came back. He's sitting next to me. I spoke with him this time. He's not from around here. He came here to go to college, but that didn't work out for him. He's asleep right now, but after he wakes up I'll be able to tell you whether he wanted a twenty-ounce vanilla crème frappe or just black coffee.

He's up.

He wants a twenty-ounce black coffee . . . and his name is Glenn.

Funny thing . . . neither of us stinks as much as we used to.

QUESTIONS ABOUT WHO YOU ARE

FOR PERSONAL STUDY AND REFLECTION: *Option 1) Find a church building that has an auditorium with stained glass windows, and do this study on a pew where you can be surrounded by stained glass. Option 2) Remembering the life of Simeon the Stylite, do this study while standing on a chair. Be sure to reflect on the feelings you have while standing on the chair.*

FOR GROUP STUDY AND DISCUSSION: *If possible, arrange for your small group to do this study in a church auditorium that has stained glass. Option 1) Before your group arrives, go to: www.wikipedia. org/wiki/List_of_saints. Search this database of "saints," choose one for each member of your group, and print out the information. As you begin the study, give a printed description to each person and allow them a few moments to familiarize themselves with the subjects. Then have them introduce their subjects to the rest of the group. Option 2) Recalling Simeon the Stylite, the monk who lived on a pedestal for more than thirty years, start your group study by encouraging everyone to stand on their chairs. Ask them to consider what it would have been like to live on a pedestal for more than thirty years. Then discuss what it really means to be in the world but not of it. After completing option 1 or 2, go through the questions and Scripture.*

1. Before you'd read this chapter, what image came to mind whenever you heard the word *saint*? Why?

2. In the Bible the word *saint* means "one who is consecrated to God." Who is the most saintlike person you've ever known? What are three of that person's best qualities?

3. Have you ever done something radical for God? What was it? What were the results? Would you do it again?

4. Realizing that all Christians are saints, what are the two biggest challenges saints have to overcome in the world today? Why?

Read Ephesians 3:14-21

---

5. According to this passage, what are some of the blessings our Father in Heaven offers to all saints?

6. Which of these are you most grateful for today? Why?

7. Since God is able to do "more than all we ask or imagine," what would you like to ask him for right now?

"Lord, I haven't always been clear on your definition of a saint. But I know that if I believe in and try to follow you, you can help me live a life through which your light can shine. That's an identity I can be proud of. Forgive me for _____

_____ ,

and help me to live a consecrated life."

YOU ARE EXTRAORDINARY

Jason, his coach, and his student body

9

> *You are the salt of the earth. But if the salt loses its*
> *saltiness, how can it be made salty again?*
> *It is no longer good for anything. . . . You are the*
> *light of the world. A city on a hill cannot be hidden.*
>
> MATTHEW 5:13, 14

> *Dear friends, I urge you, as aliens and*
> *strangers in the world, to abstain from sinful*
> *desires, which war against your soul.*
>
> 1 PETER 2:11

It happened in a gym in upstate New York. And it was recognized by ESPN at their 2006 awards show as the greatest sports moment of that year. In the final, seemingly meaningless moments of a game that was already decided, an extraordinary thing occurred.

Jason McElwain is autistic and loves basketball, but he was unable to make the team at Greece Athena High School in Rochester, New York, because he was considered too small.[1] So he settled for the next best thing: he became the team manager. Jason, or J-Mac as he's known to his teammates, had done a great job as manager, missing only one game in four years. In recognition of Jason's dedication to his job, his team, and his school, Coach Johnson arranged for Jason to dress for the last game of the year. His classmates were ready with cutouts of Jason's face on sticks; and when Jason entered the game, the gym erupted with applause. One minute after entering the game, Jason launched a three-pointer and missed terribly. Undeterred, Jason launched another three-pointer and nailed it. The fans went crazy. But he wasn't finished. Jason kept shooting and kept sinking three-point baskets, eventually hitting six three-pointers and a two-pointer for a total of twenty points!

> Within days Jason's extraordinary performance was being talked about from the White House to my house and houses around the world.

When the game was over, the fans stormed the floor and carried Jason off the court as a hero.

It was a record-setting performance and an event that captured the world's attention. Within days Jason's extraordinary performance was being talked about from the White House to my house and houses around the world. This event was extraordinary but, in my opinion, not necessarily for the obvious reasons.

Yes, it is extraordinary for a basketball player to hit six three-pointers in a game.

Yes, it is extraordinary for a basketball player with *autism* to hit six three-pointers in a game.

And I admit it is extraordinary for a basketball player with autism to hit six three-pointers in a game when he's not a basketball player at all but, rather, a manager who has not played a single minute of a single game in high school up to that point.

But it was the people involved who made this event extraordinary. It would not have happened without the extraordinary decision of an extraordinary coach, Jim Johnson. An ordinary coach might have given Jason a plaque at the end-of-the-year awards banquet in recognition of four years of service to the team as manager. An ordinary coach would not have given playing time in an actual game. What an extraordinary coach, and what an extraordinary thing to do for an extraordinary young man!

And yes, Jason is extraordinary—not just for his performance at the end of that game at the end of the season, but for his performance at every practice and every game. An ordinary young man who had not made the team might have moved on with hurt feelings and resentment. Not Jason. He volunteered to be at every practice and every game for four years to help his team—earning their trust, their respect, and their love. What an extraordinary young man!

But Coach Johnson and Jason were not the only extraordinary people in that gym. The student body at Greece Athena High School did an extraordinary thing by celebrating and honoring Jason the way they did that night. I wish everyone could experience what Jason experienced. Every person in this world deserves to have his name chanted, to have a cutout of his face put on a stick and waved in the air, to be cheered as his name is called on the PA system, to have every action on the court encouraged, and to be carried off the court as a hero. What an extraordinary student body!

Things like this don't happen every day, and we don't see extraordinary people like these every day either. But we should. God expects us to be extraordinary every day, but all too often we settle for ordinary.

If good is the enemy of great, ordinary is the enemy of extraordinary.

I don't like ordinary. I don't think ordinary. I don't *do* ordinary. Ordinary annoys me. I don't want to live an ordinary life, have an ordinary marriage, raise ordinary kids, preach ordinary sermons, serve with an ordinary church . . . and I don't want to write ordinary books. Ordinary is easy. Anybody can *do* ordinary. Anybody can *be* ordinary, which is why my dad was upset with me when I got a C on a test and then tried to justify it by pointing out that "everybody else did bad on the test too."

"You're not everybody else," Dad said. (Maybe you've heard that one too!) "You're a Chambers, and I expect more from you. We raise thoroughbreds in this house. If you want to be ordinary, you're going to have to move in with the family down the road."

"You need to remember who you are," Dad would say. "God has a plan for your life, and you need to be prepared so that when he needs you, you'll be ready."

Most young people rise to meet their parents' expectations. If parents expect their kids to fail, they probably will. And if parents expect their kids to be extraordinary, they probably will.

Ordinary was not an option in our house. Mom and Dad expected more from us, and they got it.

Dad knew I'd been given that C because I had chosen one more hour in the pool when I should have chosen one more hour at my desk. Dad knew that I was not really trying. And not really trying for long periods of time leads to a life called ordinary. I knew that Dad loved me and believed in me, so I tried harder next time; and I'm still trying harder. Daily I fight the temptation to be ordinary, but it's as if ordinary stalks me. It stalks you too.

WE HAVE A CHOICE

Every day is a series of decisions through which we define the day as either ordinary or extraordinary. Every day an African gazelle wakes up with a decision to make: to run or not to run. It knows that it must run faster than the fastest lion or it will be killed. The first day the gazelle decides not to run is the last day of its life. Every day we wake up with a decision to make too: to be extraordinary or not to be.

Kiss your spouse on the way out the door, look into her eyes, and tell her you love her—and you are outrunning ordinary. But rush out the door with a simple good-bye, and ordinary has caught you.

Hug each of your kids before they leave for school, and tell them that you love them and wouldn't trade them for all the money in the world—and you are outrunning ordinary. Keep your nose in the paper as they rush out the door, and ordinary has caught you.

> **Every day we wake up with a decision to make too: to be extraordinary or not to be.**

Tell your boss that you are grateful for her leadership—and mean it!—and you are outrunning ordinary. Tear down your boss in the break room, and ordinary has caught you.

Take the kids to soccer practice so your wife can relax before dinner—and you are outrunning ordinary. Work late when you don't have to and arrive late for dinner, and ordinary has caught you.

Have a family game night after dinner—and you are outrunning ordinary. Let the boys play video games in their room, your daughter listen to her MP3 player in hers, your wife play solitaire on the computer in the den, while you play with your sports car in the garage . . . and ordinary has caught you.

Pray with your kids before bed—and you are outrunning ordinary. Let your kids put themselves to bed while you watch *SportsCenter,* and ordinary has caught you.

Go to church, get involved with your church, give to your church, and invite others to your church—and you are outrunning ordinary. Go to church only on Christmas and Easter, and ordinary has caught you.

Build a close relationship with God through prayer, Bible study, and discipleship—and you are outrunning ordinary. *Talk* about building a close relationship with God through prayer, Bible study, and discipleship, and ordinary has caught you.

Have Jason dress, and put him in the game—and you are outrunning ordinary. Give him a plaque at the sports banquet at the end of the season, and ordinary has caught you.

I don't want to be ordinary. And I definitely don't want anyone who reads this book to reshelve it, regift it, or return it still thinking of himself as anything but extraordinary. God expects more of us.

> In comparing us to salty salt, shining lights, and cities on hills, Jesus is calling us to be extraordinary.

That's the point Christ was trying to make in that sermon on the mountainside at the beginning of his ministry. He said, "You are the salt of the earth. But if the salt loses its saltiness, how can it be made salty again? It is no longer good for anything, except to be thrown out and trampled by men. You are the light of the world. A city on a hill cannot be hidden" (Matthew 5:13, 14). In comparing us to salty salt, shining lights, and cities on hills, Jesus is calling us to be extraordinary.

During Christ's time salt was used when making sacrifices, as currency, and as a preservative for meat and fish. It was valuable because . . . well, because it was salty. It was extraordinary. But if salt were ever to lose its saltiness, it would become ordinary and worthless.

The ancients depended on daylight, as well as the limited light they managed to produce before our age of electricity. Light enabled them to work, care for the home, and simply function. Without light, their lives would have been one-dimensional and terribly hindered; but because of light, their lives were blessed. Light was an extraordinary gift. And even though we often take it for granted today, light is still extraordinary.

What makes a city on a hill extraordinary is the fact that it can be seen for miles around, especially at night when its lights are shining.

Ordinary cities are not easily seen, but extraordinary cities capture the attention of travelers and beckon them to enter in and find safety, nourishment, and rest.

We are not supposed to be ordinary. We are supposed to be extraordinary.

Before going further I feel the need clear up a few things.

First, I want to give you permission to view yourself as extraordinary. You may feel uncomfortable thinking of yourself as extraordinary, but that's just because you're thinking from the world's perspective and not God's. This is not about pride; it's about respect. When I tell you that you are extraordinary, it is not to make you prideful but respectful, both of yourself and your designer.

Second, when I say that you are extraordinary, I'm saying you are beyond what is common. You are unique. You are different, but good.

Third, when I say that you are extraordinary, I mean that God designed you to be evocative. I know that may seem like an odd choice of words. I wrestled to find the right word to express what I see in the Bible, and I chose *evocative* because it means "to bring to mind." Our lives should be so extraordinary that even a glimpse of a brief moment of our lives will bring God to mind.

The service manager for the Dodge dealer called from South Carolina to tell me that the transmission in our van was fixed and that the van was ready to be picked up. After calculating the strain of driving to Columbia, South Carolina (on the wallet, our kids, and ourselves), and after finding an inexpensive flight online, my wife and I decided that I'd fly up to get the van.

I had an early flight that morning, so we had to carry our kids straight from bed to the car for the short drive to the airport. On the way to the airport, our son Sylas noticed the sunrise. It was amazing! The eastern sky was a shade of orange I don't think I've ever seen before. Sylas was captivated by its beauty. It was extraordinary and brought God to his mind . . . and ours.

As a dash of salt brings taste to mind, the first ray of morning sunlight brings the day to mind, a city brings civilization to mind, six three-pointers from a boy with autism bring a bunch of extraordinary people to mind . . . and as a sunrise brought God to Sylas's mind, our lives should bring God to mind. When people observe our lives, they should see only a reflection of Jesus and think only about God. And they will, if we choose—each day—to be extraordinary.

WE DON'T HAVE A CHOICE

The sun can't decide not to shine. Salt can't decide not to be salty. Light can't choose not to illuminate, and cities on hilltops can't choose not to be noticed. In Christ we are extraordinary, whether we choose to be or not, which is exactly what Peter points out. He uses words that aren't as politically correct as the word *extraordinary*—but mean the same thing. In describing our extraordinary-ness, Peter uses the words *aliens* and *strangers*.

To a group of Christians who were being subjected to a severe persecution under the oppressive rule of the Roman emperor Nero, Peter wrote, "Dear friends, I urge you, as aliens and strangers in the world, to abstain from sinful desires, which war against your soul. Live such good lives among the pagans that, though they accuse you of doing wrong, they may see your good deeds and glorify God on the day he visits us" (1 Peter 2:11, 12).

What do you picture when you hear the word *stranger*? I picture the hideous, candy-offering, van-driving creep whom elementary-school students are taught to run from on the playground.

Do you know what God pictures when he hears the word *stranger*?

You.

That doesn't sit well at first. Strangers are strange, and we don't value being strange. We like to be liked. We want to fit in. We wear what everyone else is wearing, talk like everyone else is talking, laugh at all the same jokes, watch what everyone is watching on TV, go with the herd into the theater to see the latest blockbuster, and drive home to a house that looks just like every house in the neighborhood.

Strange doesn't get you a raise. Strange doesn't get you a date with the homecoming queen. Strange doesn't get your kids into the right private school. Strange doesn't get you the best table in the restaurant. Strange doesn't get you picked first for kickball. Strange doesn't get you voted Most Likely to Succeed or Most Popular.

No. Strange is most likely to get you ridiculed, avoided, and voted off the island. But that's nothing compared to what aliens get.

What do you picture when you hear the word *alien*? A green creature with big eyes, long fingers, a huge head, and evil intentions?

Those kinds of aliens don't belong. Those kinds of aliens are feared, so they must always try to convince the locals that they "come in peace." Those kinds of aliens end up in pieces on metal tables outside Roswell, New Mexico. Who'd want to be that kind of alien?

> **Do you know what God pictures when he hears the word *alien*? That's right, you. He sees you as an alien, someone beyond ordinary.**

Or maybe when you hear the word *alien*, you picture a person crammed with eighty other people on a boat off the coast of south Florida, or you picture a person dashing across a desert toward the southern border of Arizona.

Those kinds of aliens end up working bent over in fields in the hot sun, or as awkward outsiders who are tolerated but not always accepted, or sometimes even dead in the desert.

Do you know what God pictures when he hears the word *alien*?

That's right, you. He sees you as an alien, someone beyond ordinary.

Just look around. Have you seen what ordinary looks like? Ordinary looks like people living together before they're married. Ordinary looks like binge drinking at the sorority house. Ordinary uses the Lord's name as a curse word. Ordinary looks like cheating . . . on a test, on your taxes, and on your spouse. Ordinary laughs at a dirty joke.

Have you seen ordinary these days? Ordinary looks like sin.

Ordinary walks around with her cleavage displayed. Ordinary is a bigot. Ordinary tells lies to his parents. Ordinary exhibits road rage. Ordinary keeps the money when the clerk gives back too much change. Ordinary looks at pornography after his wife goes to sleep.

Have you seen ordinary these days? Ordinary looks like sin.

If we want to please God, we have no choice. We must "abstain from sinful desires" (1 Peter 2:11). We must fight back when those desires "war against" our souls (v. 11). We must "live such good lives among the pagans that, though they accuse you of doing wrong, they may *see your good deeds and glorify God* on the day he visits us" (v. 12, emphasis added).

Here's my version of 1 Peter 2:11, 12: "Live such extraordinary lives in this ordinary world that, though people think you are strange, they will see your extraordinary-ness—and God will come to mind. Then their sin will come to mind, and they will choose to be extraordinary too. Every day until the day God comes back again, they will praise him for bringing such saltlike, lightlike, city-on-a-hill-like, extraordinarily strange aliens into their ordinary lives."

You can choose to be extraordinary by submitting your life to Christ. And once you give your life to him, you'll never be ordinary again. You'll have no choice. You'll be extraordinary, whether you feel extraordinary or not.

And when that happens, people will find Jesus.

Lives will be changed forever.

Hopeless people will find hope.

And boys like Jason will be carried off the court as heroes.

QUESTIONS ABOUT WHO YOU ARE

FOR PERSONAL STUDY AND REFLECTION: *From a recent newspaper, clip an article that tells an extraordinary story. Or print an extraordinary article from an online news source. Reflect on the details of the story before beginning the questions.*

FOR GROUP STUDY AND DISCUSSION: *Ask each group member to bring an article from a newspaper (or an online news source) that contains an extraordinary story. Begin your group time by asking each person to share his or her story. Then discuss why these stories are extraordinary. Continue your study time with the questions and Scriptures.*

1. What is the most extraordinary thing you've ever experienced? Why was it extraordinary?

2. What is the most ordinary thing you experience on a daily basis? Why is it ordinary?

3. What's the most extraordinary thing you've done during the past year? What made this thing extraordinary?

Read Matthew 5:13, 14

4. What are some foods you cannot imagine eating without salt?

5. Recall a time when you were most grateful for light, and explain why.

6. Think about a time when you were most grateful for a person who was a Christian. What happened?

7. What do you think are the top three things that keep most of us from living extraordinary lives?

8. What can you do this week to be extraordinary? Be specific.

"Lord, you do extraordinary things for me all the time. This week I am committing to do the following extraordinary thing: _____ _____ _____ .

Please help me to be extraordinary for you today and forever."

YOU ARE INDISPENSABLE

"Here's the church . . ."

10

> The body is a unit, though it is made up of many parts; and though all its parts are many, they form one body. . . . In fact God has arranged the parts in the body, every one of them, just as he wanted them to be.
>
> 1 CORINTHIANS 12:12, 18

> You are the body of Christ, and each one of you is a part of it.
>
> 1 CORINTHIANS 12:27

A lot of evolutionists say that some parts of the human body are vestigial, but those evolutionists are—in my humble opinion—mistaken.

In 1893, a German follower of Charles Darwin, Robert Wiedersheim, wrote a book in which he claimed that eighty-six organs in the human

body were what he called vestigial.[1] Wiedersheim and other evolutionists believe that vestigial organs are organs that were once necessary
but are now—because of evolution—useless and no longer needed,
except to serve as visible traces of human evolution. During this time
in history, up to one hundred eighty organs were considered vesti-
gial, but since that time the purpose for most of these body parts has either become known or a secondary purpose has been discovered, rendering the body part no longer truly vestigial.

> Believing that some of these body parts were completely dispensable has led many doctors to remove them without much thought as to the consequences resulting from their absence.

Some examples of "vestigial" organs whose uses have been identified are the appendix (which we now know produces important antibodies and helps to protect our intestines from infection), the tonsils (which we now know are the first line of defense in protecting
our bodies from infection by helping to catch and filter germs that
we inhale or ingest), the vertebra at the base of our spine called the
coccyx (which we now know has two muscles attached to it that help
hold our pelvic organs in place), and the thyroid gland (which we now
know helps to control our metabolism and growth).

Believing that some of these body parts were completely dispensable has led many doctors to remove them without much thought as to
the consequences resulting from their absence. I don't have tonsils, and
I didn't really miss them until I realized how important they are to the
human body. These important filters were removed when I was very
young. As an adult I wonder how many sick days I could have avoided if
my tonsils had been available to do what they were designed to do.

My tonsils were tiny masses of tissue that became infected because
they were doing what they were designed to do: keep bacteria and

viruses from entering my body. And for that, they were cut out of my body and thrown away.

The same thing happened to my appendix. It was removed after it became infected while doing what it was designed to do. At the time, I enthusiastically agreed to its removal and utter destruction, not because it was useless but because it was painful.

Tonsils, the appendix, the coccyx, the pituitary gland, the thymus gland, the pineal gland, and all of the other "vestigial" organs are not useless. Having been misunderstood, these body parts have been considered dispensable. While it is true that we can sometimes remain healthy without them, they should not be considered useless and without purpose.

Human beings should not be viewed in that light either.

You are not dispensable.

A UNIFIED BODY

There are no useless parts in the human body. Every part of the human body is important and was not designed to be dispensed with. I believe the same is true of the body of Christ . . . and so does God. When some people act as if certain parts of the body of Christ are vestigial, they are as mistaken as the evolutionists are about human body parts.

The apostle Paul wasn't mistaken. He, writing to a divided bunch of Christians, says, "The body is a unit, though it is made up of many parts; and though all its parts are many, they form one body" (1 Corinthians 12:12).

The statement could have had quite an impact on the original readers. You see, the church in Corinth was dysfunctional. The city of Corinth was a city of half a million people. It was a commercial, trade, and cultural center, as well as the home of the temple to Aphrodite, which loomed (literally and spiritually) over the city. In Corinth, the worship of Aphrodite involved sex with one of the more than one thousand priestesses in the temple. This corrupt form of worship seemed to ooze out of the temple, down the mountain on which it sat, and through the streets below, like an insidious wave overtaking and corrupting everything and every person in the city.

This corruption seems to have entered the church in Corinth in the form of sexual immorality (1 Corinthians 5), abuse of Christian liberties (chap. 8, 10), abuse of the Lord's Supper (chap. 10, 11), disorderly worship (chap. 14), disbelief in the resurrection of Christ and the future resurrection of believers (chap. 15), and intense division (chap. 1, 3, 6, 12).

> **Division, like a cancer in the body of Christ, is a tool that Satan uses to attack the church.**

One of the first evidences of sin in a church is division, and like one cancer cell, it must be dealt with before it grows into something that can kill the body.

Division, like a cancer in the body of Christ, is a tool that Satan uses to attack the church. He considers you to be a vestigial organ in the body of Christ. He wants you to be removed when you become infected by the consequences of sin. He rejoices when you are dissected and discarded, because his only goal is for the body of Christ to be lying in pieces on the floor, waiting to be incinerated in the fires of Hell—one useless piece at a time.

So Satan organizes cliques in the church.

Satan gossips.

Satan makes his presence known at angry church board meetings.

Satan's favorite phone calls begin with the words, "Did you hear what (*insert name of church member here*) did?"

Satan criticizes the leadership behind their backs.

Satan stirs up dissension.

Satan masks lies about another Christian as a prayer request.

Satan is a skilled musician who can divide a traditional church with an electric guitar, a contemporary church with an organ, and an a cappella church with any instrument.

Satan complains to the church leadership about "the kind of kids" the youth leader is reaching, wondering aloud, "Do we really want to attract those kids? Isn't there someplace else they could go?"

Satan's dream is for you to be standing on one side of the church while other Christians stand on the other, pointing at you with hate in their hearts.

Satan and his demons celebrate when a church splits.

Satan smirks when he reads in the paper that the local church is closing its doors for good.

Satan loves it when parts of the body of Christ are regarded as useless. But . . . no part of the body of Christ is useless.

You are not a vestigial organ in the body of Christ.

Please don't believe what that person said about you.

Please don't be discouraged when someone ignores you.

Please don't stop looking for a church that will accept you, embrace you, and love you.

You are not useless.

No, you are indispensable. But before you (and I) get a big head, I need to point out that although we are indispensable, we are not as indispensable as Christ, the only one who can legitimately have a big head, because he *is* the big head. And the body of Christ must have the head.

Mike lived for eighteen months without a head.[2]

Mike was only five-and-a-half-months old and living in Fruita, Colorado, when Lloyd Olsen tried to cut off his head and succeeded . . . but failed at the same time. Clara, Lloyd's wife, had sent Lloyd out to get Mike ready for dinner, which, considering that Mike was a wyandotte rooster, meant cutting off his head.

Lloyd caught Mike, held him down, and swung the ax—cutting off Mike's head. But Mike seemed unfazed and continued walking around the yard. He acted as if nothing were wrong . . . Mike, that is. So Lloyd—impressed by Mike's will to live—started to feed him grain and water with an eyedropper. This proved to be a successful method, and Mike grew in both weight and notoriety, quickly becoming the "Wonder Chicken" and capturing the attention of the public as he and Lloyd undertook a nationwide tour. Tragically, Mike died in a hotel room while on tour (like other well-known celebrities have been known to do!), after living for eighteen months without a head.

Mike managed without a head, but the body of Christ cannot.

Churches that remove Christ from their teaching, preaching, worship, terminology, and focus are decapitating themselves and will eventually die. Without Christ it is impossible to have, and be, the body of Christ.

Christ, as the head (Ephesians 1:22; Colossians 1:18), is indispensable because he gives his body life; we are indispensable because we give his body functionality. Christ needs us to fulfill the role in the body for which we have been created; there is something he needs us to do. As Paul points out, "The eye cannot say to the hand, 'I don't need you!' And the head cannot say to the feet, 'I don't need you!'" (1 Corinthians 12:21).

Christ needs you.

How does that sound to you?

Do you feel needed right now?

Do your kids act as if you're an embarrassment?

Does your wife act as if your role in your kids' lives is to stay out of the way?

Does your husband seem interested in you only when he's in the mood for physical intimacy?

Has your boss stopped asking for your input on the big projects and the smaller ones too?

Have your friends stopped asking you for advice?

Has your offer to fill the Sunday school class teacher position been ignored?

Do you feel that your church wants your money but not you?

Are you sick of eating alone, talking to yourself, and not being able to drive in the carpool lane because you are always by yourself in the car—and in your life?

Has Satan been whispering into your soul, "You are dispensable"?

Satan's a liar who wants to isolate you *here*

> **Satan's a liar who wants to isolate you *here* so you'll be isolated *there* for all eternity.**

so you'll be isolated *there* for all eternity. You must not allow him to remove you from the rest of the body of Christ. You were designed to be placed in the body of Christ for a specific purpose.

A SHARED PURPOSE

The apostle Paul knew what he was talking about when he said, "The body is not made up of one part but of many" (1 Corinthians 12:14). The human body is made up of many parts, and every part serves a purpose.

There are 206 bones in the body, unless you're a newborn baby; a newborn baby has 300–350 bones, depending on which source you read. There are 650 muscles in the body.[3] The normal human body has ten toes, ten fingers, two eyes, two ears, one mouth, one nose, plus two arms and two legs. There is one brain, one heart, two kidneys, one small intestine, one large intestine, one pancreas, one liver, and a pair of lungs. Everyone has one appendix. (Well . . . *you* may have one appendix.)

And if you count our cells (the average adult is made up of one hundred trillion cells) and the rest of our body parts, we have at least 100,000,000,000,898 body parts![4]

And each one is important!

Just ask my four-year-old son, Sylas.

As we were preparing for a trip to visit some friends in Jacksonville, Sylas fell off the bed. By the way he was crying, we thought one of his 206 bones was broken. But after some testing of his mobility, we realized that he had just pinched a nerve in his neck. This microscopic bundle of nerve fibers we call *a* nerve kept my boy immobile and in tears for most of the day.

> You can choose to face the challenges of this world with all of the power your body can muster, or you can face this world with all of the power *his* body can muster.

Nerves are small but important, carrying signals from the brain that keep every part of our body functioning and in coordination with the brain. You may feel small and insignificant, but you are an important vessel through which Christ can carry his message of love to a hurting world.

I have to stop here and say a couple of different things to the non-Christian readers and Christian readers.

To my non-Christian readers: You are important to God. You were designed by God for a specific role in his body, but you have to choose to fulfill that role. God does not add people to his body by force and against their wills—like some sort of mad doctor who steals random body parts and recklessly reassembles them in his dark laboratory into a malformed creature who is doomed to stagger through the back alleys of life, horrifying all who gaze upon his hideous appearance.

No. God wants to add you to his body gently, carefully, lovingly, and precisely. He wants you to want to fulfill his destiny for your life as an indispensable part of his body. But it's your choice. You can choose to face the challenges of this world with all of the power your body can muster, or you can face this world with all of the power *his* body can muster.

To my Christian readers: I'm really not trying to convince you that you are a part of the body of Christ. In Christ, you *are* a part of that body, whether you think you are or not. What I'm trying to do here is convict you so that you'll begin fulfilling your role in the body of Christ—because you're needed! Paul wrote, "The eye cannot say to the hand, 'I don't need you!'" (1 Corinthians 12:21). And it's the truth. I need you and you need me to do what we were designed to do; otherwise our combined inaction will lead to the body of Christ being crippled, or totally paralyzed.

Figure out your part in the body of Christ and embrace that role with confidence and contentment. If you are a foot, don't say, "Because I am not a hand, I do not belong to the body" (1 Corinthians 12:15). And if you are an ear, don't say, "Because I am not an eye, I do not belong to the body" (v. 16). Remember that "God has arranged the parts in the body, every one of them, just as he wanted them to be" (v. 18).

Don't say "I'm just . . ." or "I'm not . . ." or "I can't . . ."

Just say "I will."

My friend Jeanne lives in almost constant pain. Jeanne suffers from rheumatoid arthritis that has twisted her hands and has made it painful to walk; yet she walks and she serves and she loves. She is a member and a vibrant part of the body of Christ at Southside Christian Church. Jeanne and her husband, John, do the jobs that we can't find anyone else to do, and they do these with smiles on their faces. On Sunday mornings I can count on Jeanne to greet me with a smile as she sets out the bulletins (that she and John copied and folded) and sets up the decorations she's prepared for our coffee corner.

Christ can count on Jeanne too. Though her body is disabled, Jeanne refuses to disable the body of Christ by not fulfilling her purpose. She realizes, in ways that we could not understand, that each part of the body has a purpose. But she also realizes that the body of Christ would be weaker if she viewed herself as a "weaker" part of Christ's body. Paul says it this way: "On the contrary, those parts of the body that seem to be weaker are indispensable" (1 Corinthians 12:22).

Jeanne is indispensable to me, to Christ, and to his body. She may be physically weak, but the body of Christ is spiritually strong because of people like her who work to help the church fulfill its purpose.

SHARED PAIN AND PLEASURE

It was going to be a good service.

The room was set up. I was doing a series on ministry, and the day's sermon was entitled "The Requirements for Ministry." The songs for the song service were arranged, and things were going exactly as we had planned . . . until we realized that God had other plans.

Earlier that week, a young mother—who desperately wanted children—delivered her twins only twenty-six weeks into the pregnancy. Tammy and her husband had to watch as their little boy died five minutes after birth and their little girl died twenty-six hours later. They felt an indescribable pain that was all the more poignant because only a year earlier they had lost a baby girl who'd lived for only one day.

The service began as planned. But as we started to sing about the love of God, Tammy and her husband, Richie, who were sitting close to the front, began to cry. Those around them began to cry, and the body of Christ began to respond spontaneously.

Sensing the leading of God, we changed our plans and submitted to God's—stopping the service, gathering around this grieving couple, and bathing their pain with prayer and their heartache with love. We prayed for them. We hugged them. We cried with them. We did what bodies do.

A healthy body shares both pain and pleasure, and a healthy church body must do the same. Paul reminds us that "God has combined the members of the body . . . so that there should be no division in the body, but that its parts should have equal concern for each other. If one part suffers, every part suffers with it; if one part is honored, every part rejoices with it" (1 Corinthians 12:24-26).

Tammy and Richie are a part of the body of Christ, and I am a part of the body of Christ; their suffering is my suffering, and their joy is mine too. With the successful births of their two boys and beautiful little girl in the years since that tragic experience, we have shared their joy as well. Richie and Tammy—and every other person who is a part of the body of Christ at Southside—are indispensable, so we commit to being indivisible, which has led to joy indescribable.

I heard a story about a girl named Jamie who refused to go to school or church for an entire year after losing her arm in an accident. Jamie felt bad about herself and started to wonder if a one-armed girl could really be of any use to God. She even started to doubt that God had a purpose for her life. She wondered if her life really mattered that much to anyone.

Eventually she decided that it was time to face her friends in her Sunday school class at church. Knowing that this was going to be a difficult experience, her mother called the Sunday school teacher and asked that he not call attention to Jamie, which the teacher agreed to. But when he got sick on Sunday and had to call a substitute, he forgot to tell the second teacher about Jamie's situation.

At the end of the lesson that day, the substitute teacher led the class in doing the hand motions to the familiar children's poem: "Here's the church, and here's the steeple. Open the door, and see all the people." Everything was going as planned until Jamie began to cry because this simple task was now impossible for her.

Sensing Jamie's suffering and the leading of God, one of her class-mates submitted to God's plan, knelt beside Jamie, extended one of his hands, entwined his fingers in hers, and—together—they said, "Here's the church, and here's the steeple. Open the door, and see all the people."

In that moment, Jamie realized that in allowing herself to believe that she was useless to God, she had been very much mistaken.

QUESTIONS ABOUT WHO YOU ARE

FOR PERSONAL STUDY AND REFLECTION: *Work through this time of study and reflection in a place where you will be able watch people walk by (a park, mall, or sidewalk café). List some of the differences you notice in people.*

FOR GROUP STUDY AND DISCUSSION: *Begin your study time by doing an activity that is exactly the opposite of the hit TV show* Survivor. *Sit in a circle. Place a chair in the middle. Encourage each member to take a turn sitting in the chair as everyone else in the group shares why this person is needed in the group and why the person should* not *be voted off the island. Then as a group, study and discuss the questions and Scripture.*

1. Have you ever been disabled by an injury? What happened? How did you feel while disabled?

2. Has there ever been a time when you felt indispensable? dispensable? Why did you feel this way?

Read 1 Corinthians 12:12-27

3. If you had to describe yourself as a part of the human body, what part would you be, and why?

4. If, in fact, it is God's desire for everyone to be part of the body of Christ, what part do you think God created you to be? Why?

5. Paul makes it clear that no part of the body of Christ is dispensable. Do you think there are some parts in the body of Christ that are not as appreciated as others? If so, which ones are appreciated less? Why is that?

6. How do you make people feel needed? What can Christians do to make every part of the body of Christ feel needed?

7. In your opinion, which is easier for members of any group to share: pain or pleasure? Why?

8. When has a member of the body of Christ helped to share your pain? Describe how this experience impacted you.

9. Is there a common purpose at the church you attend? If so, what do you think it is?

10. What is your life purpose?

"Lord, sometimes I haven't felt needed. I'm so glad that your plan is for everyone to be an indispensable part of an important group, the body of Christ. Help me realize that I'm indispensable, and help me to make other people feel indispensable too."

YOU ARE A CHILD OF GOD

"I wish you were my little girl."

*In love he predestined us to be adopted
as his sons through Jesus Christ,
in accordance with his pleasure and will.*

EPHESIANS 1:4, 5

*You did not receive a spirit that makes you a slave
again to fear, but you received the Spirit of sonship.
And by him we cry, "Abba, Father." . . . Now if we
are children, then we are heirs—heirs of God
and co-heirs with Christ, if indeed we share in his
sufferings in order that we may also share in his glory.*

ROMANS 8:15-17

I've been thinking about my dad today.

This August, like each August since 1988, brought mixed emotions.

Most of the people in my family were born in August, so we have birthdays to celebrate, which makes August fun. August is also when kids in Florida go back to school, family trips are over, and everyone is focusing on the activities that fill each autumn. I love the energy and excitement that come with August, but it has been a difficult month for me and my family since my father's death on August 8, 1988.

Today is August 8.

The anniversary of my dad's death is not getting easier. I miss him so much. He died before I was married. He was gone five years before the birth of the first of my four kids. I'd love to have even one more day with him. I dream about him a lot, but in my dreams he's not the same. He usually sits in the corner of the room or stands on the perimeter of my dreams and doesn't say much. He's always glad to be there—I can tell—and I'm always so happy to see him.

Just thinking about him right now releases a flood of bittersweet memories through the valley of my soul, and I once again find myself forced to make one of three choices: ride the wave of emotions past countless pleasant memories, resist the wave by refocusing my thoughts on some innocuous project, or surrender to the wave and allow grief to carry me away to wherever it wants me to go.

Although Dad's been gone for almost twenty years, I've found that he can be back in an instant if I hear a song he used to like or a Scripture he enjoyed preaching about . . . or if I run into one of his old friends or see my son standing with his arms folded just like Dad used to do or notice my daughter trying to hold a spoon on her nose just like Dad used to do.

Yes, I miss my dad. And I think I'll miss him just as intensely every August this side of Heaven.

If I could have one more day with my dad, I don't know what we'd do. But I can promise you, not one minute would be wasted. I'd tell him a million times that I love him. I'd drink a cup of coffee with him, even though I hate coffee, because he loved coffee but died before I was really old enough to go out to the local diner for a cup of coffee. There's not anything I wouldn't give to have a cup of coffee with him and have him tell me about Heaven. I'd introduce him to my kids and tell him why I'm so proud to be their daddy and why I'm so grateful he was mine. I'd ask him a ton of questions about how to raise teenagers, since my tour of duty as a father of teenagers is coming sooner than I'd like and I feel so unprepared.

I'd hug him and study his face, guaranteeing that I won't forget even the slightest wrinkle after he's gone again. I'd tell him that he was such a great dad and I'm thankful every day for

> **If I could have one more day with my dad, I don't know what we'd do. But I can promise you, not one minute would be wasted.**

the nineteen years I had with him as his son.

Toward the end of our day, I would thank him for everything he did to bless my life and prepare me to be a man of God, a good husband, and father. We'd have to find a basketball court so we could play one more game of H-O-R-S-E. And afterwards, as we sat in the grass catching our breaths, I would try to find the right words to thank him for things he said to me that gave me security and a clear sense of identity.

I'd thank him for telling me to "remember who you are" and for saying that if he had to pick a son from all the boys in the world, "I'd pick you to be my son every time." And I'd be sure to mention the times he reminded me that he wouldn't trade me "for all the money in the world."

What an amazing thing for a father to say.

There's a lot of money in the world. In fact, according to estimates, there is approximately six trillion dollars in the United States alone.[1] That means that I was worth more than six trillion dollars to my father, which makes a boy feel pretty good, even when he's older and has boys of his own now.

My father's love for me gave me a profound and powerful sense of identity.

Do you know that God wouldn't trade you away for all the money in the world either? Not because he doesn't need the money (which he doesn't), but because he loves you more than you could ever imagine.

His love for you should give you a profound and powerful sense of identity.

ADOPTED

In Christ, you and I are God's children, not because we chose him, but because he chose to adopt us through Jesus Christ. Paul writes, "He chose us in him before the creation of the world to be holy and blameless in his sight. In love he predestined us to be adopted as his sons through Jesus Christ, in accordance with his pleasure and will" (Ephesians 1:4, 5).

The adoption process has always intrigued me because it's an opportunity to be like God.

The adoption process has always intrigued me because it's an opportunity to be like God. My wife and I considered adoption a few years ago after struggling with infertility for several years. When we thought we couldn't have any more children, we began the adoption process. But about halfway through the initial interview and application phase, my wife got pregnant, so we didn't continue with our plans for adoption. We were excited about having another child of our own, but we were also a little disappointed because we'd been looking forward to adopting a child of our own. Adoption is divine in a way that giving birth can never be, and my wife and I had been eager to experience what God experiences each time someone comes to Christ.

For the past year I've been thinking about adoption. Not because we're considering adopting another child—which we actually are—but because we adopted a dog from a local pound almost a year ago.

He's a dachshund-labrador mix. Don't laugh. He's two years old. Black. Big ears. Short legs. Long nose. That's the long . . . and short of it . . . uh, of *him.*

We had gone to the pound on a quest to find a priceless dog at a cheap price. The kids really wanted a dog. They're old enough to both play with and enjoy a dog; my wife and I are old enough to know better. But our love for the kids clouded our good judgment, and we started looking for the perfect pet. We don't have a fenced-in backyard, so we knew the dog would have to be indoors. And we have four kids, so we knew the dog would have to be unbreakable. Our last dog was struck by lightning, so we knew the dog would have to be well-grounded. A dachshund made sense.

We picked him up after he endured a very important procreation-ending procedure. Afterwards, he seemed a little sore and pessimistic about the future, even though our selection of him changed his life. Before we came along, he was living in a cage, where he had lots of fresh air, rainwater, and barking neighbors—but he had very little hope. We selected him from the midst of his prison and spent a week preparing a place for him. He had no idea that he was soon to have a new bed, new toys, new bowls for food and water, new collar, new family . . . and a new name!

We named him Cooper, which has to be better than what he was called before; he didn't have a name. The people at the pound were probably calling him Spot, Samson, Jo Jo, or Number 19 (because he was living in cage number 19 at the pound). My daughter Ashton came up with the name Cooper . . . after the Mini Cooper . . . the car. (I don't know . . . you'll have to ask my daughter, or better yet, ask *your* daughter.)

Cooper's life changed for the good the moment we adopted him.

He was no longer a stray; he was a part of our family. He was adopted. He now belongs. He did nothing to deserve it, except look cute, lick my kids' faces, and not yap in our presence. We couldn't wait to bring him home for good, and I mean *for good* in both senses of the term.

It's been good for him.

New home.

New life.

New name.

During this past year with Cooper, I've done some thinking about you and me. It hasn't been a completely smooth transition from Cooper's life in the pound to life as a part of our family. As I mentioned in chapter 1, he has submission problems; but what I didn't mention is that he also has bladder-control problems. This year has not just been rough on me, it's also been rough on our living room furniture, which Cooper has marked too many times to count.

At those times when Cooper relieves himself on my bare feet while I'm too late trying to hook him to a leash so I can take him out, my wife reminds me to be patient with Cooper because God is patient with us. It started out as a joke, but the more I think about it, the more I realize that she's right.

Like Cooper, Christians have been rescued too. Humans *will* stray from home and find themselves trapped in a prison called sin. Then one day . . . a nice man with loving eyes, wide smile, broad shoulders, thick hair, and nail-scarred wrists hears our whimpers and doesn't walk by or look away. He kneels down, reaches his hand out through the bars, examines our mangy exteriors, smiles, and says, "I'll take him. I'll take her."

In Christ, you and I were adopted. We were rescued.

New home.

New life.

New name: Christian.

We were no longer strays. We belonged.

Adoption is amazing because it creates bonds between strangers that are as strong as—if not *stronger* than—the bonds that exist between parents and children connected through blood. If you don't believe me, just find some parents of adopted children and ask them how much they love their adopted children and whether they would love them any more if they shared the same DNA.

It's been my experience that the bond between adoptive parents and their children is exceedingly strong. Often, these parents who adopt have been unable to conceive a child and have endured many years of heartache and disappointment, so the child they adopt is not just a part of their family but also the answer to a prayer, the fulfillment of a dream, and a blessing beyond words . . . which is exactly how God feels about us.

> The child they adopt is not just a part of their family but also the answer to a prayer, the fulfillment of a dream, and a blessing beyond words . . . which is exactly how God feels about us.

When we come to Christ and are adopted by God, we are an answer to a prayer, the fulfillment of a dream, and a blessing beyond words. The word that Paul uses to describe what God feels toward all his adopted children is *pleasure* (Ephesians 1:5).

When I was a child, I knew a lot about God. My parents kept God in the center of our lives and taught me about him constantly. But I didn't really *know* him until—through adoption—I became his son. Then I had the pleasure of getting to know him, on my own, through an intimate relationship called faith. And in getting to know him, I have learned how much our existence, worship, obedience, and membership in his family bring him pleasure. Now he's no longer just a mysterious old man, sitting in a fancy room way up in the sky somewhere really far away, whom I'm trying not to anger so he doesn't get mad and smite me. He's my *Abba,* my Father.

SONS AND DAUGHTERS

Paul uses this word *abba* in his letter to the Romans. He writes, "You did not receive a spirit that makes you a slave again to fear, but you received the Spirit of sonship. And by him we cry, '*Abba*, Father.' The Spirit himself testifies with our spirit that we are God's children" (Romans 8:15, 16).

Now I know this is not very spiritual, but ever since I've written the word *abba*, I've been singing "Dancing Queen" because when I hear the word *abba*, the first thing that comes to mind is the Swedish pop group that had a string of hits in the '70s and '80s. The second thing that comes to mind is the loving face of my heavenly Father, which should be the first image that comes to all of our minds at the sound of that word, because there are no orphans in God's family.

> It's true that he is a jealous God who covets our undivided attention. But he is also our *Abba*—our Daddy.

This word *abba* is an intimate Aramaic term that is similar to the word *daddy* in English.[2] It's a name used by a child for a father that reflects the familiarity and love common in a healthy child/father relationship. In the context of Romans 8:15, 16, Paul is reminding the Christians in Rome that, in Christ, they are not slaves who need to be afraid that the sin they are struggling to overcome can't be defeated; they are not destined to stand before an angry God. Rather, they are sons who can cry out to God for help in their time of sin in the same way a son would cry out to his daddy.

In those verses Paul is trying to combat the enslaving spirit of fear. He chooses a word that emphasizes an aspect of God's person that sometimes is overshadowed by the verses that teach us that our Father in Heaven is a "jealous God, punishing the children for the sin of the fathers to the third and fourth generation of those who hate" him (Deuteronomy 5:9). It's true that he is a jealous God who covets our undivided attention. But he is also our *Abba*—our Daddy—who will spend an afternoon cleaning out our wounds after we slide into sin, graciously saying, "I'm so sorry, son. I know this hurts, but your wounds won't heal properly unless I get all the dirt out."

In the park behind our house a couple of months ago, I heard my son crying, "Daddy! Daddy!" I was sitting on a nearby bench reading, but I quickly put my book down and ran to him. I found him standing in a fire ant hill, and he had ants all over his shoes and socks. Fire ants have a painful bite that leaves mosquito-like sores behind. I immediately picked him up and began swiping the ants off his legs and feet, all the while reassuring him, "Daddy is here. It's going to be OK."

He didn't need a judge. He needed to be rescued.

He didn't need my wrath. He needed my love.

He didn't need a disciplinarian. He needed an *abba*.

The Christians to whom Paul was writing found themselves standing in their "sinful nature," and without help they were going to die (Romans 8:13). Paul urged them to cry out *"Abba*, Father" because he knew that if they did, their loving Daddy would rescue them before it was too late.

This loving Daddy doesn't just let his sons and daughters face temptation without giving them a way of escape (1 Corinthians 10:13).

This loving Daddy doesn't ignore them when they cry out to him from bondage in Egypt (Exodus 3:9).

This loving Daddy would go through a dumpster to save you. So if you feel like you're in a hopeless situation, cry out to your *Abba*.

You may feel alone right now, but you are not an orphan.

You may feel angry right now, but you are not an orphan.

You may feel afraid right now, but you are not an orphan.

You may feel abandoned right now, but you are not an orphan.

Through Christ you and I can become children of God. And as children of God, we have an *Abba,* a Father, who is the Almighty. He has both the power and desire to protect us and provide for us . . . now and for all eternity.

HEIRS

In Romans 8, as Paul finishes his thoughts on God as our *Abba* and us as his children, he throws in one more wonderful truth. He writes, "If we are children, then we are heirs—heirs of God and co-heirs with Christ, if indeed we share in his sufferings in order that we may also share in his glory" (Romans 8:17).

> We're not just children of an amazing Father in Heaven; we are also heirs to all of his riches and glory.

Wow! We're not just children of an amazing Father in Heaven; we are also heirs to all of his riches and glory.

Grandpa Maxey always told his grandchildren that we were "heirs to the Maxey millions"; and when I was seven years old, I actually believed it. I thought Grandpa was a millionaire. I knew he was a minister and the president of a college in Kentucky devoted to training African-American men and women for ministry, which I thought meant he was rich. Now I understand that his occupations only meant that he was unpopular in the circles in which you must be popular if you have any dream of ever making enough money to support your family in ministry. It seems that wealthy Christians in the late 1950s were not always eager to financially support cross-cultural evangelism in the South, so Grandpa and Grandma Maxey knew the joy of living on faith and the generosity of the faithful. Now that they have gone to their reward, they know the joy of living in glory with a generous Father.

They never owned a large house . . . but now they own a heavenly mansion.

They never lived on Easy Street . . . but now they live on streets of gold.

They never had a lot of possessions on earth . . . but now they have treasures in Heaven.

Jesus said, "Do not store up for yourselves treasures on earth, where moth and rust destroy, and where thieves break in and steal. But store up for yourselves treasures in heaven, where moth and rust do not destroy, and where thieves do not break in and steal" (Matthew 6:19, 20). Think how amazing a reward would have to be to be considered a "treasure" in Heaven. That's exactly what you and I will inherit as heirs of God if we are faithful even to the point of death (Revelation 2:10).

My first car was my first treasure. It was a 1972 green Ford Maverick. I loved that car and spent a lot of time and money on it. Now that car is in a dump somewhere, as flat as a pancake. As much as it hurts to say it, "the Mav" is a rusty piece of trash—and so is so much of the junk that we spend our lives working for.

Eternal life is my last treasure.

I read an article about a man named Stanley S. Newberg. Mr. Newberg fled persecution as a Jew and came to America, where he made a good living. When he died at age eighty-one, his estate was valued at 8.4 million dollars, of which he gave 5.6 million in cash to . . . guess . . . that's right: the US government! He was so grateful to the country that took him in, in his will he left most of his wealth to a bureaucracy that daily spends that much money in just under two minutes.

Why would Mr. Newberg want to give so much money as an inheritance to a group of people who seem so undeserving?

Well, Mr. Newberg did it for the same reason that God offers his glorious wealth, eternal life, and blessings beyond imagination as an inheritance to a group of people who seem just as undeserving—it's his will.

God loves us. We are his children, and he has a great inheritance waiting for us as a part of his will. So don't lose heart.

You may not own a large house . . . but you will own a heavenly mansion.

You may not live on Easy Street . . . but one day you are going to live on streets of gold.

You may not have a lot of possessions . . . but one day, if you are faithful to your *Abba* Father until your very last breath, you will have treasures in Heaven.

> You are his child, an heir, and he wants you to know that he wouldn't trade you for all the money in the world.

You are his child, an heir, and he wants you to know that he wouldn't trade you for all the money in the world.

What about us? Would we trade an eternal relationship with God for all the money in the world? I hope not.

I read a story that reminded me how much our Father in Heaven loves us. Well-known author and counselor John Trent tells how a Mrs. Leonard turned an ordinary hearing test into an extraordinary event in the life of one little girl.

Mary had grown up knowing that she was different from the other kids, and she hated it. She was born with a cleft palate and had to bear the jokes and stares of cruel children who teased her non-stop about her misshaped lip, crooked nose, and garbled speech.

With all the teasing, Mary grew up hating the fact that she was "different." She was convinced that no one, outside her family, could ever love her . . . until she entered Mrs. Leonard's class.

Mrs. Leonard had a warm smile, a round face, and shiny brown hair. While everyone in her class liked her, Mary came to love Mrs. Leonard.

In the 1950's, it was common for teachers to give their children an annual hearing test. However, in Mary's case, in addition to her cleft palate, she was barely able to hear out of one ear. Determined not to let the other children have another "difference" to point out, she would cheat on the test each year. The "whisper test" was given by having a child walk to the classroom door, turn sideways, close one ear with a finger, and then repeat something which the teacher whispered.

Mary turned her bad ear towards her teacher and pretended to cover her good ear. She knew that teachers would often say things like, "The sky is blue," or "What color are your shoes?"

But not on that day. Surely, God put seven words in Mrs. Leonard's mouth that changed Mary's life forever. When the "whisper test" came, Mary heard the words: "I wish you were my little girl."[3]

God loves us and longs for each of us to become his children, his heirs.

Just look up and listen up. He's looking at you and saying something you need to hear. Can you hear him? He's speaking to you and saying, "I wish you were my little girl" or "I wish you were my little boy."

What an amazing thing for the Father to say.

QUESTIONS ABOUT WHO YOU ARE

FOR PERSONAL STUDY AND REFLECTION: *Find a picture of yourself as a child. Reflect on what your life was like at the time the picture was taken. If you could go back in time and speak to yourself at the moment this picture was taken, what would you say?*

FOR GROUP STUDY AND DISCUSSION: *Ask group members to bring childhood pictures that include their families. Have them introduce their families, briefly describing each family member and their roles in the family. Then use the Scripture and questions to guide discussion.*

1. What is one of the fondest memories you have from your childhood that involves one or both of your parents?

2. What color best describes your childhood? Why?

3. What color best describes the relationship between your parents and yourself today? Why?

4. Was your father a significant presence in your childhood? If your father was involved in your life when you were a child, what was one of the most important things he ever did for you?

5. What was one of the most important things your father ever said to you?

6. Think of some characteristics of your heavenly Father. Which are your favorites?

_____

Read Romans 8:15-17
_____

7. Have you ever inherited something? What was that experience like?

8. What is one thing that you once considered a treasure in your life that you now consider as trash? What changed?

9. What are some rewards the heavenly Father promises in Heaven? Which would you most look forward to receiving? Why?

10. What one thing can you do this week to help other people understand that they have the opportunity to be adopted by God through Christ?

"Lord, thank you for loving us so much that you would choose to adopt each of us—all of us—and make us your children. What an honor it is that we can address the Creator of the universe as Abba. *I want to declare my love for you in the following ways:* _____

_____

_____

_____ ."

YOU ARE A PRIEST

Help for the hen

12

*You are a chosen people, a royal priesthood,
a holy nation, a people belonging to God, that you
may declare the praises of him who called
you out of darkness into his wonderful light.*

1 PETER 2:9

*To him who loves us and has freed us
from our sins by his blood, and has made us
to be a kingdom and priests to serve
his God and Father—to him be glory and power.*

REVELATION 1:5, 6

Perhaps you're familiar with the story of *The Little Red Hen.* . . .

A little red hen once found a grain of wheat. "Who will plant this wheat?" she asked.

"I won't," said the dog.

"I won't," said the cat.

"I won't," said the pig.

"I won't," said the turkey.

"Then I will," clucked the little red hen.

So she planted the grain of wheat. Soon the wheat began to grow, and the green leaves came out of the ground. The sun shone and the rain fell, and the wheat kept on growing until it was tall, strong, and ripe.

"Who will reap this wheat?" asked the little red hen.

"I won't," said the dog.

"I won't," said the cat.

"I won't," said the pig.

"I won't," said the turkey.

"Then I will," clucked the little red hen.

So she reaped the wheat.

"Who will thresh the wheat?" asked the little red hen.

"I won't," said the dog.

"I won't," said the cat.

"I won't," said the pig.

"I won't," said the turkey.

"Then I will," clucked the little red hen.

So she threshed the wheat.

"Who will take this wheat to mill to have it ground?" asked the little red hen.

"I won't," said the dog.

"I won't," said the cat.

"I won't," said the pig.

"I won't," said the turkey.

"Then I will," clucked the little red hen.

So she took the wheat to mill, and by and by she came back with the flour.

"Who will bake this flour?" asked the little red hen.

"I won't," said the dog.

"I won't," said the cat.

"I won't," said the pig.

"I won't," said the turkey.

"Then I will," clucked the little red hen.

So she used the flour to bake a loaf of bread.

"Who will eat this bread?" asked the little red hen.

"I will," said the dog.

"I will," said the cat.

"I will," said the pig.

"I will," said the turkey.

"No, I will," clucked the little red hen. And she ate the loaf of bread!

Perhaps you're familiar with this story as well. . . .

A little country preacher wanted to conduct a church service. "Who will help me make the bulletins?" he asked.

"I won't," said the busy businessman.

"I won't," said the retired schoolteacher.

"I won't," said the avid golfer.

"I won't," said the homemaker.

"Then I will," said the little country preacher.

So he gathered information for the announcements, chose songs for the service, typed the information into the bulletins, printed the bulletins, and folded the bulletins so they'd be ready for the service. But then he looked around and noticed that the church building was dirty.

"Who will help me clean the church building?"

"I won't," said the busy businessman.

"I won't," said the retired schoolteacher.

"I won't," said the avid golfer.

"I won't," said the homemaker.

"Then I will," said the little country preacher.

So he went to the supply closet, secured the cleaning supplies, and began cleaning the church building. Some old bulletins and scraps of paper, on which a child had doodled, were scattered on one of the pews and needed to be thrown out. The baptistery water was cold and cloudy, and the toilet in the men's restroom was clogged. In the racks on some of the pews, he noticed last week's Communion cups that should be tossed, which reminded him that he needed to get Communion ready for the service.

"Who will help me prepare Communion for the service?"

"I won't," said the busy businessman.

"I won't," said the retired schoolteacher.

"I won't," said the avid golfer.

"I won't," said the homemaker.

"Then I will," said the little country preacher.

So he wiped down all of the Communion trays, carefully placed the bread in the bread trays, and poured the juice into the tiny cups. On his way to carry the trays to the refrigerator, two children nearly collided with him, which reminded him that he needed to find some teachers for Sunday.

"Who will help me teach the new Christians' class, the adult Sunday school class, the midweek Bible study, the small group that meets at my house, and Sunday night youth group?"

"I won't," said the busy businessman.

"I won't," said the retired schoolteacher.

"I won't," said the avid golfer.

"I won't," said the homemaker.

"Then I will," said the little country preacher.

So he prepared a lesson for every class, but before he could finish, it was Sunday morning and time for the service.

"Who will attend this church service?"

"I will," said the busy businessman.

"I will," said the retired schoolteacher.

"I will," said the avid golfer.

"I will," said the homemaker.

"But I won't," said the little country preacher, "because I have an ulcer, my hair is falling out, I can't sleep, I have no appetite, my wife stopped talking to me a month ago because I'm never home at night, my kids hate me and this church because it monopolizes my time, my dog won't come when I call because he doesn't recog-

> **"This stress of trying to do God's work by myself is causing me to have chest pains!"**

nize me, I have to get a second job because we can't survive on what you pay me, and I'm on my way to the hospital because this stress of trying to do God's work by myself is causing me to have chest pains!"

May I confess something to you?

I'm a preaching minister. I come from a long line of ministers, as I mentioned earlier. Additionally, I have four brothers-in-law in ministry, and my father-in-law is a minister. I know many ministers. But none of that is what I want to confess to you.

What I want to confess to you is that it felt really good to write what I wrote in those paragraphs above. I think more people should know what a lot of ministers in smaller churches—and some that are not that small—have to do each week to prepare for a typical Sunday service.

It felt good to point out that too many of these ministers are having to do the work of the church almost completely by themselves because church members think "it's their job" and "it's what they are paid to do."

IT'S EVERYBODY'S JOB

Yes, it is their job—and what they are paid to do (though in some cases it hardly qualifies as pay)—but it's also *our* job because all Christians are priests.

Did you know that?

Under the old covenant the role of the priests was crucially important to the spiritual health of the nation of Israel. Priests, acting as mediators between God and his people, would enter the Lord's presence to offer gifts and sacrifices. But with the death of Jesus, this sacrificial system was abolished. With his death and resurrection, Jesus became our high priest and mediator (Hebrews 8:1; 9:15), and through

> God never meant for the work of his church to become a one-man show.

him all Christians now function as priests—bringing our gifts and sacrifices into the Lord's presence on our own and through our mediator Jesus Christ.

In the New Testament it's clear that there are different roles in the church. And as those roles are fulfilled, each member of the body of Christ should find both work and purpose. Paul writes, "It was he who gave some to be apostles, some to be prophets, some to be evangelists, and some to be pastors and teachers, to prepare God's people for works of service, so that the body of Christ may be built up" (Ephesians 4:11, 12).

God never meant for the work of his church to become a one-man show. Leaving one person to do all the work of the church can weaken a church, making both the minister and the members vulnerable to satanic attacks.

Satan surely likes it when one person is expected to fulfill all the work of the church by himself, or herself, because Satan longs for a majority of the body of Christ to be immobilized. Satan prefers to have to deal with only one man at a time.

One man can do only so much by himself, so he's less of a threat. It's easier to attack one man. And in churches that are built on the work of one man, Satan knows that if he can bring down that one man, he can potentially bring down—or slow down—many more.

One man brings only one set of ideas and one strategy to his ministry, so he's more predictable.

One man is easier to discourage. Just ask Henry Jones's wife.

One sunny Sunday morning, Henry Jones awoke to find his wife standing over him, shaking him by the shoulder.

"You must get up," she urged. "We have to get ready for church."

"I don't want to go to church," he replied. "I want to stay in bed."

Crossing her arms over her chest, his wife demanded, "Give me three good reasons why you should stay in bed and not go to church."

"OK," he answered. "First, I don't get anything out of the service. Second, I don't like the people there. And third, no one there likes me. Now can you give me three good reasons why I *should* go to church?"

His wife responded, "First, it will do you some good. Second, there are people who really do like you, and they'll miss you if you aren't there. And third, you're the minister!"

One man is easier to trap in sin when he is isolated in a ministry by himself with little or no accountability. Just ask any of the former ministers' wives I know whose husbands are no longer in the ministry—or in their homes—because they gave in to the temptations of sexual sin.

Satan knows that if he can get one man to do the work of God while the rest of us sit and watch, he maintains the strategic advantage. So we must remember who we are and do what God has planned for us to do.

Everyone who is in Christ is a priest with a job to do. We must seek to do the job well. But we must also seek to do it purely.

PURITY

Peter writes, "You are a chosen people, a royal priesthood, a holy nation, a people belonging to God, that you may declare the praises of him who called you out of darkness into his wonderful light" (1 Peter 2:9). He points out that when we become Christians, we become priests. In becoming both, we leave—or should I say, it is *assumed* that we have left—the "darkness" and enter into "his wonderful light." It is important for us to remember that to be an effective priest, we must strive to be pure.

> It has always been important for priests to be godly and to set an example of purity.

Each of us, through Christ, has been called "out of darkness into his wonderful light" to call others out as well. So we must strive to live pure lives; if we fall we are liable to hurt more than ourselves.

Child-abuse scandals have rocked the Roman Catholic Church in the past few years. In the ensuing arrest and imprisonment of priests, we have all seen that sin in the life of a priest has a negative impact on the reputation of the priest himself, the priesthood, and the church in general. Satan hath no joy like the image of a priest in handcuffs on national TV. Similar unfortunate situations have occurred as high-profile evangelists have been exposed as embezzlers, adulterers, and tax evaders.

Priests, as servants of God, have always been looked to as role models, so it has always been important for priests to be godly and to set an example of purity. But under the old covenant, priests were not just role models; they were representatives of God who stood—every day—before God on behalf of the people. And of all the days priests represented God's people, on no day was that representation more important than the Day of Atonement.

The Lord set aside the tenth day of the seventh month as a day of atonement for the sins of the children of Israel (Leviticus 16:29-33). This day was set apart by God as an opportunity to roll back the sins of the people by offering forgiveness for the sins of the previous year. The high priest was set apart to facilitate this process. He had to prepare carefully to make sure that he was worthy to be used by God for this special purpose.

The Day of Atonement was an opportunity for the people of God to be made pure, and since the high priest played a key role in this ceremony, his personal purity was of the utmost importance and needed to be addressed first. God wanted his high priest and his people to understand the importance of personal purity. So on the Day of Atonement, the high priest took five baths and participated in ten washings to make sure that he was pure physically and spiritually. Before he could confess the sins of Israel, he had to confess his own sins and the sins of his household.

Imagine what could happen in churches around this world if every minister took such efforts to be personally pure before encouraging others to do the same. Imagine what could happen if every Christian took such efforts to be personally pure before fulfilling his or her responsibilities.

Pure priests have a powerful testimony.

Pure priests have credibility.

Pure priests, who are willing to sacrifice themselves to God as living sacrifices, are instruments that God can use to make every day a day of atonement for sinners everywhere.

The Day of Atonement was not an ordinary day for a priest, and today must not be an ordinary day for you and me either. We are priests, and before we begin fulfilling our mission each day, we must make our personal purity a priority, not just for our sake, but for the sake of those in need of atonement and out of respect for the Atoner whom we serve.

In Revelation, John points out that the Lord "has made us to be a kingdom and priests to serve his God and Father" (Revelation 1:6). And later in this book he writes, "You have made them to be a kingdom and priests to serve our God, and they will reign on the earth" (5:10), which points out that, as priests, it is not just enough to be pure; we must also be productive. We are priests because there is work to do.

RESPONSIBILITY

Yes, when you and I give our lives to Jesus Christ, we become priests.

God does not make us priests so that we can sit around in fancy clothes in our air-conditioned sanctuaries, feeling good about ourselves and relishing how important and valuable we are to the overall functionality of the church.

No. You and I are priests because there is work to do. According to the verses we just read from Revelation, a priest's job is to serve God.

> **Imagine what could happen in this world if every Christian remembered that, in Christ, we are priests.**

Unemployment can break the spirit and embitter the soul, so praise God that he has more for us to do than just sit in a pew, stare at a minister, and listen to a sermon he took all week to prepare—while we secretly think it should be better, considering it was "the only thing he had to do all week."

Imagine what could happen in churches around this world if every Christian showed up not to be entertained, but to join the leadership in serving God.

Imagine what could happen if every Christian remembered that, in Christ, we are priests—"ordained" at our baptisms to serve God.

Imagine what could happen in the lives of lost people if the royal priesthood would realize that serving God looks like being pure, being faithful to your spouse, mowing a widow's yard, discipling your kids, obeying God's commands, giving cheerfully, protecting the weak, changing diapers in the nursery, helping the poor, teaching the junior high boys' Sunday school class, counseling a young married couple, mentoring the son of a single mother, cleaning the church restrooms, and telling lost people about Jesus.

Perhaps you're familiar with the story. . . .

God created an incredible universe and filled it with beauty and life. He created beings in his image, put them in a beautiful garden on one of the planets, gave them free will, and hoped that they would use it wisely. God placed many trees in the garden, but told the beings that there was one from which they could not eat. They chose to eat from it, but it did not satisfy them. In fact, it killed them . . . eventually; and it has led to the death of multitudes of people from spiritual hunger ever since.

God decided enough was enough and that it was time to satisfy spiritual hunger and save the souls of the people he created, so he prepared a way for them to live. He sent Jesus, the bread of life (John 6:48).

Then he asked, "Who will help me take the bread of life to my people so they can live forever?"

"I will," said his priests.

QUESTIONS ABOUT WHO YOU ARE

FOR PERSONAL STUDY AND REFLECTION: *To begin, write down the name of a minister you know. List a few of his responsibilities. Consider what difficulties he might encounter in carrying out those duties and what sense of reward he might have as well. If you're a Christian, write down your name and list a few of the responsibilities you have as a Christian.*

FOR GROUP STUDY AND DISCUSSION: *Ask a minister and his wife to join your group. Make them the guests of honor for dinner. After dinner, create an opportunity through which the members of your group can thank them for some of the things they do that are a particular blessing. Use the questions—and the minister's answers—to help group members correct any misconceptions they may have had about the role of minister/priest. Close your session with a time of prayer for the minister and his family.*

1. In your opinion, what are the best and worst aspects about being in the ministry as a full-time occupation?

2. List the top ten things—in order of time required—that you think a minister does for the church in any given week.

3. When has a minister done something that was a real blessing to you? What was it?

Read 1 Peter 2:9, 10

4. Based on these verses, who are we in Christ? Which of the descriptions Peter uses is the easiest to accept? Which is the hardest to accept? Why?

5. When you hear the word *priest,* what is the first thing you usually think of? Why?

6. In your opinion what is the best aspect of belonging to the "royal priesthood"? Why?

7. How should the understanding that all Christians are priests change what we do at church on a typical Sunday? How should this understanding change what we do during a typical week away from church?

8. If you are a Christian, what is one specific thing you can do this week to fulfill your responsibilities as a priest?

"Lord, thank you for the chance to study this topic. I haven't always clearly understood that you not only want me to be a member of your body, your church, but you also consider me a priest. That makes me feel important! Help me to be pure in the following areas: _____

_____

and purposeful in these areas: _____

_____

_____ *."*

YOU ARE AN OVERCOMER

Forget the duck!

13

> *Who is it that overcomes the world? Only he who believes that Jesus is the Son of God.*
>
> 1 JOHN 5:5

> *I heard a loud voice in heaven say: "Now have come the salvation and the power and the kingdom of our God, and the authority of his Christ. For the accuser . . . has been hurled down. They overcame him by the blood of the Lamb."*
>
> REVELATION 12:10, 11

His story is one of the greatest comeback stories I've ever heard.

His name was James J. Braddock, but you may recognize him by the name given to him by the well-known New York newspaperman and writer Damon Runyon, who dubbed Braddock, Cinderella Man.[1]

Braddock's life is the story of a man who overcame extraordinary odds to achieve a great victory. From where we sit in history, we may regard his life as a fairy tale; but from where he sat in history, it probably seemed more like a nightmare.

Being born and raised in a poor Irish home in Hell's Kitchen in New York City during the early 1900s gave Braddock a toughness that would serve him well throughout his life. He was a boxer who turned professional at the age of twenty-one—achieving moderate success, but he ultimately hurt his hand in a championship fight in 1929, which essentially ended his career. He tried to regain his boxing prominence, but finished out his career winning only eleven of the next thirty-three bouts.

He was victimized, but he was no victim.

By this time, America was deep into the Great Depression. Braddock did extremely difficult work as a laborer on a dock. He fought hard to keep this job so that he could continue to provide for his wife, Mae, and their three children.

He was discouraged. He was broken and he was broke. To provide the necessities for his family during this dark period in his life, Braddock even accepted relief from the government in the form of welfare, which he promised to repay as soon as he could.

He was victimized, but he was no victim.

In 1934, Braddock's life was changed forever when he was offered a chance to begin a comeback in a fight against a boxer named John "Corn" Griffin, who viewed Braddock as an easy victim and the door to great publicity. Braddock was supposed to be a stepping-stone but ended up being a stumbling block, upsetting Griffin and reviving Braddock's own career. In the next year Braddock won several other key fights and ended up with a shot at the heavyweight championship of the world against the champion, Max Baer.

Max Baer was a huge and powerful man. He had accidentally killed boxer Frankie Campbell in the ring with only two hits that dislodged

Campbell's brain within his skull. Baer viewed Braddock as an easy payday. Braddock viewed Baer as his family's ticket out of poverty. As the movie based on Braddock's life (*Cinderella Man*) accurately showed, Baer was fighting for money; Braddock was fighting for milk.

On June 13, 1935, Braddock shocked the world by defeating Max Baer and becoming the heavyweight champion of the world in one of the biggest boxing upsets of all time. Braddock's victory made him a hero to people all over the world and allowed him to provide for his family and repay the government every penny he had received while on welfare.

Braddock was a winner who continued fighting and made it known that he didn't plan on losing anytime soon. In fact, he made it clear that he wanted his hand raised in victory in his final fight.

Braddock's last fight was in 1938, when he came from behind to win a unanimous decision in what is considered by boxing historians to be the best performance of Braddock's career. At the end of the fight, to signify Braddock's victory, his hand was raised into the air just as he had always wanted.

Yes, he had been victimized, but he refused to be a victim and went out as a victor.

Life comes with problems.

Sometimes we create problems for ourselves.

A few years ago, I read about a forty-six-year-old man in Taiwan who jumped into a lions' den at the Taipei Zoo.[2] It seems that he was trying to convert the lions to Christianity, repeatedly shouting, "Jesus will save you!" This is a little ironic because he ended up needing to be "saved" himself, from himself, by the zoo workers who drove away the lions with water hoses and tranquilizer guns. The zoo workers said that if the lions had not been fed earlier in the day, this man would have been devoured, which I think would have provided him with an excellent opportunity to explain to Jesus—face-to-face—what in the world he was thinking!

Yes, sometimes we face problems of our own creation, but sometimes we face problems that hit us out of nowhere while we're minding our own business.

You and your kids are on the way home from seeing a movie, when a drunk driver crosses the double-yellow line and hits your car head-on.

You get a late-night phone call from your sister saying your mother's just been rushed to the hospital.

You get an angry e-mail from a close friend when you thought everything was OK.

Your teenage daughter tells you she's late—and she's not talking about breaking curfew.

A check bounces unexpectedly.

The doctor says, "We got your test results back and there are some irregularities, so I need to speak with you."

Your husband returns home after a long business trip and says, "We need to talk."

You're two months pregnant and spotting blood.

A policeman knocks on your door.

You think you've been called into the boss's office because you've been with the company for twenty-five years and you're up for one more raise before you retire. But instead, he fires you and gives you the morning to clean out your office.

You're working in the middle of nowhere in the middle of the night in Yellowstone National Park, when a park ranger calls and asks you to call your mom. She tells you that your dad died while preaching in Ohio yesterday and you need to come home.

Jesus said, "In this world you will have trouble" (John 16:33). But we really don't know what he means. When Jesus says "trouble," we picture minor things like disappointment, discouragement, a small paycheck, dinner with a mother-in-law, or being called names like "right-wing fundamentalist wacko." We picture unreceptive lost people who refuse to open their front doors to us. We definitely don't picture hungry lions and wooden crosses.

But that's exactly what Jesus was saying.

In John 16 Jesus spoke "plainly" (v. 25) to his disciples. He was about to be crucified, and they were about to feel deserted. But Jesus wasn't going to let this "trouble" catch them by surprise, so he tried to

> **Problems are going to come, troubles with a capital *T*, but we have a choice. We can choose to be victims, or we can choose to be victors.**

give them peace by warning them that problems were on the way. Jesus knew that his followers would be victimized, but he does not want us to be victims. Problems are going to come, troubles with a capital *T*, but we have a choice. We can choose to be victims, or we can choose to be victors.

VICTIM

May I confide in you? The thing about me and victims is this: I have heartfelt sympathy for first-, second-, or even third-time victims, but I have almost no sympathy for what I call career victims.

First-, second-, and third-time victims are those people who are hit by an unexpected tragedy, accident, or natural disaster that puts them in a position of needing food, housing, medical care, clothing, and money in order to survive until they can get on their feet again. But career victims are a different story. Career victims are those pitiful souls who are of sound mind and sound body but who have made a career out of playing the victim. They feel entitled to be taken care of for the rest of their lives by the church, by the government, or by their families.

I'm not talking about good people who need constant assistance and care just to survive. I'm talking about people who have found a way to take advantage of good people so that they don't have to take responsibility for their own lives and poor choices.

I'm all in favor of supporting victims of natural disaster for as long as it takes to help them get back on their feet again, but I am not in favor of sending them checks every month for the rest of their lives.

I'm in favor of paying someone's rent and electric bill to help him through a hard time, but I have a hard time when the "hard time" becomes *all* the time.

The ministers I know are all in favor of listening to problems and offering counsel—several times if needed. But it starts to feel like a waste of time when the counselees don't listen to counsel and keep repeating the same mistakes over and over again, leading to the same problems over and over again, prompting a call to set up another appointment for help . . . again.

People have to want to help themselves. Sometimes it seems like people create crises in their lives because they like to play the victim role. Perhaps it makes them feel important, and they like the attention. Maybe it feels good when other people come in and take care of their problems, because that means they don't have to take responsibility for their own actions.

I love people. My wife and I have enjoyed helping people in need over the years, but there's a point when enough is enough and people have to put on their big-boy and big-girl pants and do what it takes to overcome.

The most frustrating thing about encountering *Christians* who are career victims is this: I think career victims are losers, and I know that Jesus did not die on a cross so that you and I would be losers, but so that we would be overcomers.

If anyone could have played the victim card, it was Jesus.

His mother was an unwed pregnant teen.

He was born in a barn.

His cousin was beheaded shortly after his ministry began.

He never owned his own home.

His life and safety were threatened throughout his ministry.

He was hated by a number of important people and was rejected by many of his own countrymen.

He was going to be deserted by his best friends at his biggest point of need.

He was going to be judged unfairly.

He was going to be mocked, spit on, and beaten.

He was going to have a crown of nails rammed onto his head.

He was going to have to carry a cross through Jerusalem and in front of jeering people who had once cheered for him.

He was going to be nailed to a cross and die for people who didn't seem to care.

And still, he says to his disciples on the last night of his life, "I have told you these things, so that in me you may have peace. In this world you will have trouble. *But take heart! I have overcome the world*" (John 16:33, emphasis added).

Jesus was about to be victimized, but he refused to be a victim. He declared that no matter what this world did to him, no matter how many problems he had to face, no matter how many troubles came his way . . . he was a victor who had already overcome the world.

Notice that he was not talking about a coming victory but a realized victory. Jesus did not say "I *will* overcome the world" or "I *might* overcome the world" or "I *hope* I can overcome the world." No. He said, "I *have* overcome the world."

Since Jesus has won the war already, you can refuse to lose the battles you face each day. You will be victimized, but don't become a victim. Become a victor!

VICTOR

The Bible is not just inspired; it's also inspirational. The Bible is full of real stories of real people who overcame real problems.

Abram brought trouble on himself by lying to Pharaoh, telling him that Sarai was his sister and not his wife (Genesis 12:10-20), but he overcame that mistake and became the father of faith.

Joseph was thrown by his brothers into a well. Then they sold him into slavery, where he worked his way up to a powerful position in his master's home—until the master's wife falsely accused him of trying to seduce her. He was imprisoned again, where he stayed until he impressed Pharaoh with his power of dream interpretation and ended up overcoming everything (Genesis 37–50).

As an infant, Moses escaped the genocide of Israelite baby boys when his mother put him in a basket and floated him down the river (Exodus 2). He overcame his reluctance and fear of speaking (Exodus 4:10) to become one of the greatest leaders of all time.

Rahab was a prostitute who overcame a poor career choice and ended up being on the roll call of the faithful in Hebrews 11—listed in verse 31, right between Gideon and the Israelites who felled Jericho.

And speaking of Gideon, he overcame impossible odds and—with God's power—defeated one hundred twenty thousand Midianites with only three hundred men (Judges 6–8).

Hannah overcame bitterness of soul due to the barrenness of her womb and ended up being the mother of Samuel (1 Samuel 1), who would be directed by God to anoint David as king of Israel.

And in the New Testament we read of more overcomers.

Mary and Joseph overcame the challenges of giving birth to and raising the Son of God in a world that was not receptive to him.

The Samaritan woman overcame her sin and gave her entire town the opportunity to come to faith in Jesus (John 4:39-42).

Peter overcame his denial of Jesus to preach the first gospel message (Acts 2).

And Paul overcame . . . well, let's just read it from 2 Corinthians 11:23-27:

I have worked much harder, been in prison more frequently, been flogged more severely, and been exposed to death again and again. Five times I received from the Jews the forty lashes minus one. Three times I was beaten with rods, once I was stoned, three times I was shipwrecked, I spent a night and a day in the open sea, I have been constantly on the move. I have been in danger from rivers, in danger from bandits, in danger from my own countrymen, in danger from Gentiles; in danger in the city, in danger in the country, in danger at sea; and in danger from false brothers. I have labored and toiled and have often gone without sleep; I have known hunger and thirst and have often gone without food; I have been cold and naked.

Paul also had an annoying and mysterious problem he referred to as "a thorn in my flesh" (2 Corinthians 12:7).

Your story can be the story of an overcomer too, if you refuse to allow your problems to victimize you twice.

We all will be victimized at least once in our lives. This world is fallen. Problems are bound to fall on you and me sometime or another, but we must not allow those problems to victimize us again and again.

Other people may define us by our mistakes, but God does not define us by our mistakes or by our weakest moments.

We must find a way to overcome them. You *can* keep your troubles from victimizing you to the point where your realized victory could go unrealized in your life.

Don't let your mistakes define you.

Other people may define us by our mistakes, but God does not define us by our mistakes or by our weakest moments. Take Peter, for example. He denied knowing Jesus at the very time Jesus needed him the most, but Jesus refused to allow Peter to be a career victim to his momentary weakness. Jesus allowed Peter to confess his love for him exactly three times (once for each denial) and used him to be the first preacher at the very first church service ever!

We are all sinners, and we will all make mistakes. But we must not allow those mistakes to victimize us repeatedly, denying us the victory we've already won in Christ (or the victory that you *can* win if you'll choose to make Christ your Savior).

But there are probably many of you who feel beyond the reach of the grace of God.

You may feel as if your mistakes are too heinous to forgive.

You may feel like you're not worth it.

You may be reading this right now, convinced that you're no better than your worst sin.

In *Will Daylight Come?* Richard Hoefler tells the following story:

A little boy visiting his grandparents was given his first slingshot. He practiced in the woods, but he could never hit his target. He went back to Grandma's back yard, where he spied her pet duck. On an impulse he took aim and let fly. The stone hit, and the duck fell dead. The boy panicked. Desperately he hid the dead duck in the woodpile, only to look up and see his sister watching. Sally had seen it all, but she said nothing.

After lunch that day, Grandma said, "Sally, let's wash the dishes." But Sally said, "Johnny told me he wanted to help in the kitchen today. Didn't you, Johnny?" And she whispered to him, "Remember the duck!" So Johnny did the dishes.

Later Grandpa asked if the children wanted to go fishing. Grandma said, "I'm sorry, but I need Sally to help make supper." Sally smiled and said, "That's all taken care of. Johnny wants to do it." Again she whispered, "Remember the duck." Johnny stayed while Sally went fishing.

After several days of Johnny doing both his chores and Sally's, finally he couldn't stand it. He confessed to Grandma that he'd killed the duck. "I know, Johnny," she said, giving him a hug. "I was standing at the window and saw the whole thing. Because I love you, I forgave you. I wondered how long you would let Sally make a slave of you.[3]

Don't buy Satan's lies.

You may have cheated in the past, but that doesn't mean you'll always be a cheater.

You may have stolen in the past, but that doesn't mean you'll always be a thief.

> **God's grace *is* amazing, and it covers *all* our sins!**

You may have lost your virginity in the past, but that doesn't mean you can't ever be pure.

You may have been abused in the past, but that doesn't mean you are eternally "damaged goods."

You may have lied in the past, but that doesn't mean you'll always be a liar.

You may have used drugs in the past, but that doesn't mean you will always be a user.

You may be deep in sin right now, but that doesn't mean you can't be saved.

God's grace *is* amazing, and it covers *all* our sins!

Believe this.

Embrace this.

Otherwise, Satan will make you a career victim by continually whispering in your ear, "Remember the duck!"

To try to keep you from putting your faith in Christ and making him the Lord of your life, Satan will whisper in your ear, "Remember the duck!"

To try to keep you from agreeing to lead that small group, Satan will whisper in your ear, "Remember the duck."

To try to keep you from accepting God's calls to ministry, Satan will whisper in your ear, "Remember the duck."

> **The death of Jesus on the cross and his resurrection from the dead mean that you and I are no longer victims, but victors.**

When God leads you to a wonderful Christian who would make a great spouse, Satan will try to convince you that you've been too immoral to deserve such a good person, whispering in your ear, "Remember the duck."

If you've lost your virginity and vowed to be pure, but you're being tempted to drift away again (and Satan wants you to), he'll try to convince you that you're too weak to be strong and that you've done too many unholy things to ever be holy again. So he whispers in your ear, "Remember the duck."

God wants you to be victorious, but Satan wants you to be a victim. So every time God offers you grace, Satan is going to try to get you to reject it by convincing you that you don't deserve it. He'll whisper in your ear, "Remember the duck."

It's time for this nonsense to end!

The cross of Jesus means everything. It means that God loves you and sent his Son to die on that cross for your sins, even when he knew all about them already. The cross of Jesus means that you and I are forgiven. The death of Jesus on the cross and his resurrection from the dead mean that you and I are no longer victims, but victors.

God's Word is clear that in Christ and through his blood we are overcomers:

- "They overcame him by the blood of the Lamb and by the word of their testimony; they did not love their lives so much as to shrink from death" (Revelation 12:11).

- "To him who overcomes, I will give the right to eat from the tree of life, which is in the paradise of God" (Revelation 2:7).

- "He who overcomes will not be hurt at all by the second death" (Revelation 2:11).

- "To him who overcomes and does my will to the end, I will give authority over the nations" (Revelation 2:26).

- "He who overcomes will, like them, be dressed in white. I will never blot out his name from the book of life, but will acknowledge his name before my Father and his angels" (Revelation 3:5).

- "Him who overcomes I will make a pillar in the temple of my God" (Revelation 3:12).

- "To him who overcomes, I will give the right to sit with me on my throne, just as I overcame and sat down with my Father on his throne" (Revelation 3:21).

- "He who overcomes will inherit all this, and I will be his God and he will be my son" (Revelation 21:7).

So overcomer, don't let your mistakes define you!

Forget the duck!

And there's another thing you can do to prevent your troubles from keeping you outside the victory God has already secured for you: don't let your mistakes stop you.

God has a plan for your life. He created you—all of us—to do something specifically for him. Don't let anything, including sin, stop you from doing what God has called you to do.

After listing the names of many faithful overcomers (Hebrews 11), the writer of Hebrews tells us what to do to ensure that we join them in their victory. He says: "Therefore, since we are surrounded by such a great cloud of witnesses, let us throw off everything that hinders and the sin that so easily entangles, and let us run with perseverance the race marked out for us. Let us fix our eyes on Jesus, the author and perfecter of our faith, who for the joy set before him endured the cross, scorning its shame, and sat down at the right hand of the throne of God. Consider him who endured such opposition from sinful men, so that you will not grow weary and lose heart" (Hebrews 12:1-3).

Satan will try to use our sins as a noose to hang us, a snare to trip us, and a barrier to stop us, but we must not allow that. We must not quit. We must remember who we are and why we are here.

> **We must remember who we are and why we are here.**

We don't have to figure out where it is God wants us to run. God already has a plan for each life and a direction in which he'd like us to go. The Hebrews writer points out that the racecourse is already "marked out for us." We just have to run and refuse to stop—or be stopped by "everything that hinders"—until we reach Jesus. And when we find Jesus, we will find ourselves.

In one of my favorite scenes from the movie *Cinderella Man*, Mae Braddock—who went to only one of Jim's bouts early in his career—came to visit him in the locker room before his championship fight with Max Baer. Knowing that he was in the fight of his life and that he couldn't win without her support, Mae expressed her love and confidence in Jim by saying, "Maybe I understand, some, about having to fight. So you just remember who you are . . . you're the Bulldog of Bergen, and the Pride of New Jersey, you're everybody's hope, and the kids' hero, and you are the champion of my heart, James J. Braddock."[4]

Whether you know it or not, you're in the fight of your life. So you just remember who you are. You're an overcomer.

QUESTIONS ABOUT WHO YOU ARE

FOR PERSONAL STUDY AND REFLECTION: *Before going through the questions and Scripture reading, watch the movie* Cinderella Man. *(Note that this movie is rated PG-13 for boxing violence and language.) You'll also need extra paper.*

FOR GROUP STUDY AND DISCUSSION: *Option 1) Select a few clips from the movie* Cinderella Man *to show as you begin your study. Ask the group to discuss their feelings about the scenes they watched. Option 2) Begin your study time by playing a brief game in which you have one clear winner. After the game, ask the losers and the winner to describe how they feel now that the game is over. After doing option 1 or 2, work through the questions and Scripture reading together. For questions 9 and 10, provide extra paper. Allow group members to keep secret what "ducks" they wrote down. Lead the prayer time as best suits your group. You may want to place the trash can in the center of the room.*

1. What is the biggest victory you've ever been a part of? Why does it stand out to you?

2. What was the biggest defeat you've ever been a part of? What happened?

3. What are some of the biggest lessons you learned from each experience?

Read Revelation 2:7, 11, 17, 26; 3:5, 12, 21; 12:10, 11; 21:7

4. When have you felt like an overcomer? Why? Were you a Christian at the time?

5. When have you felt *overcome*? What was the difference between these two experiences?

6. Of all the rewards God promises to overcomers in the verses we read, what one reward would you most anticipate? Why?

7. Have you ever been victimized? How did that feel? How did you overcome that problem?

8. What three lessons have you learned about overcoming trials?

9. What is the "duck" you need to forget? Write it down and fold up the paper.

10. Pray, using the sample prayer given here if you like. Then throw your "duck" into a trash can.

   "Lord, thank you. When I overcame _____
   _____
   (specific problem or situation) *in the past, I realize you were there helping me. Help me now to forget the 'duck' that Satan is trying to use to keep me down. As I dispose of this paper, I pray that you will help me to both remember who I am and to forget this 'duck.'"*

ONE MORE THING TO REMEMBER

I've always loved fairy tales.

I think it's because so many fairy tales are stories of the release of extraordinary men, women, boys, girls, and animals who have been trapped in ordinary, or even oppressed, lives.

Cinderella is the story of a girl who is denied her rightful place in the family and is forced to be a servant to her evil stepmother and stepsisters. One day, with the help of her fairy godmother, Cinderella is released from her dreadful situation, given an extreme makeover—gown and glass slippers included—and attends a royal ball, at which the prince sees her for who she really is and falls in love with her. At this point, she has to run home because it's almost midnight, but in her haste she leaves a glass slipper behind. The prince, in love with the woman who wore the glass slipper but unaware of who she is, begins a kingdom-wide search to find the foot that fits the slipper. Despite continued abuse and deceit from her stepmother and stepsisters, Cinderella gets a chance to try on the slipper. It fits. An extraordinary girl is released from a harsh life, and she and the prince live happily ever after.

The Frog Prince is the story of a prince who is turned into a frog and remains trapped in a frog's body. But he is befriended by a selfish princess who eventually changes and falls in love with him. She shows him an extraordinary love and kisses him, which breaks the spell and releases an extraordinary prince who had been trapped in an ordinary frog's body. And they both live happily ever after.

Snow White is the story of a beautiful princess who doesn't know she is both beautiful and the daughter of a queen who died while giving birth to her. Her father marries another woman. This woman becomes jealous of Snow White's beauty when she asks her mirror, "Who is the fairest one of all?" and the mirror answers, "Snow White." The stepmother orders a hunter to take Snow White to the woods and kill her. Instead, he releases her, and she ends up living with seven dwarfs in a house in the woods. When her wicked queen stepmother finds out that she's still alive, she disguises herself, goes to the woods, and tricks Snow White into eating a poison apple that causes her to fall into a deep sleep. Snow White is released from the spell when a handsome young prince falls in love with her and awakens her with love's first kiss. This extraordinary princess is released from her painful life to become who she really was all along—and lives happily ever after.

There's a common theme in these stories: each of the victims was already a victor when the story began. Cinderella, the Frog Prince, and Snow White were extraordinary from the very beginning. They were victimized and trapped in unsatisfactory lives, but that wasn't the end of the story. In these fairy tales, extraordinary people were released from the lives in which they had been held captive . . . and ended up living happily ever after.

Let me see if I can make my point with one more fairy tale.

The Ugly Duckling is the story of a swan who ends up being raised by a dysfunctional and verbally abusive mother duck. She doesn't know that she's raising a swan; she just thinks she's raising a really ugly duckling, because he looks so much different than her other children. Unwisely, she allows his siblings to criticize him and peck at him and eventually admits that she wishes he had never been born.

The baby swan, not realizing who he really is and convinced that he is ugly and unloved, begins a dangerous journey, during which he is almost shot by hunters, almost bitten by a dog, and almost frozen to death in a pond.

Many days into his journey, he sees three beautiful white swans and decides to risk his life by approaching them. They were so beautiful, he was drawn to be with them, even though he felt so ugly. As he approached them he bowed his head to them, expecting death, but two incredible and unexpected things happened. The first was that they didn't kill him. They accepted him as one of their own, swimming around him and stroking him with their beaks. But the second thing was even more unexpected.

When he bowed his head to the other swans, he saw his own reflection in the water and no longer saw himself as an ugly gray bird. He saw the reflection of a beautiful swan. He couldn't believe it. Up to this point his life had been miserable, and his destiny seemed grim. He had been laughed at, picked on, and treated horribly. But now, he was happy to have endured such trouble. With the realization of who he really was, everything—including his destiny—had changed.

The moral of this fairy tale—and a truth that we must always remember—is found in a line toward the end of the story, which reads, "It matters not to have been born in a duck-yard, if one has been hatched from a swan's egg."[1]

You may have been convinced by the people in your duck-yard that you are ugly, unwanted, and unloved. But God wants you to know that you are not an ugly duckling. You have been hatched from a swan's egg.

You may have been victimized by an abusive father who tried to convince you that you were too weak to do anything meaningful with your life. But God wants you to know that you are not an ugly duckling. You have been hatched from a swan's egg.

You may have been victimized by a tragedy, a bad relationship, or a problem that came out of nowhere, and you feel defeated and that you have no hope of ever overcoming the terrible situation in which you find yourself. But God wants you to know that you are not an ugly duckling. You have been hatched from a swan's egg.

You may look at your reflection in the mirror and see an ugly duckling. Maybe you've made a long series of bad choices, and you've allowed Satan to convince you that you aren't any better than your worst mistake. But God wants you to know that you are not an ugly duckling. You have been hatched from a swan's egg.

You are a swan.

You are an extraordinary person who may have been trapped in an ordinary or troubled or brutal life. Once you realize your true identity, you can unleash the power God has designed in you.

It's not a fairy tale. God created you, loves you, and sent his Son to die for you. He believes wonderful things about you. So it's time for you to wake up, put on the glass slipper, rescue the princess, go to the ball, slay the dragon . . .

Be the hero or heroine God planned for you to be. Look at the reflection of your life in God's Word, and start living happily ever after as you remember who you are!

QUESTIONS ABOUT WHO YOU ARE

FOR PERSONAL STUDY AND REFLECTION: *Visit the children's section of your local library or dig through your kid's closet for a fairy-tale book. Then spend some time reading a few fairy tales before beginning this time of personal study.*

FOR GROUP STUDY AND DISCUSSION: *Option 1) Begin group time by reading aloud your favorite fairy tale. Option 2) Since this is the last study of this book, why not do something really special, like throwing a costume party? Ask group members to come dressed as characters from their favorite fairy tales. Their choices can help you decide how to steer some of the questions. Questions 7–10 will help members review and will provide important takeaway.*

1. What is your favorite fairy tale? Why?

2. If you were writing your own fairy tale, what would the story be about? Why?

3. Has your life ever felt like a fairy tale? When, and how?

4. Have you ever felt like an ugly duckling? What happened?

5. Have you ever felt like a beautiful swan? What caused you to feel this way?

Read John 3:16

6. How should this verse make you feel about yourself? Why?

7. As you reflect on this book, what is the one thing you remembered about yourself that was the most encouraging?

8. We've looked at many Scriptures throughout this study. Is there one Scripture that best describes something you want to strive for next week? Take a few moments to find it and note it.

9. Which of the thirteen "you are" statements (the chapter titles of this book) will be the hardest to remember about yourself? Why?

10. What have you learned during the reading of this book that you think will be the most helpful during the next week? year? decade? Why?

"Lord, thank you for reminding me of who I am. I know that you created me to be extraordinary. I know that I was born to fly, so please release me from living an ordinary, unfulfilled life. I know it's possible! If I stay close to you, I will soar in you and for you. Help me to do that. Amen."

NOTES

BEFORE WE START

[1] Kim Murakawa, "Man Found Face Down on Beach Has Amnesia," Honolulu *Star-Bulletin,* May 2, 1996, www.starbulletin.com/96/05/02/news/story2.html (accessed August 14, 2006).

[2] Debra Barayuga and Harold Morse, "Man with Amnesia Learns Name, Family," Honolulu *Star-Bulletin,* July 17, 1996, www.starbulletin.com/96/07/17/news/story3.html (accessed August 14, 2006).

CHAPTER 1

[1] Charles Darwin, *The Descent of Man and Selection in Relation to Sex,* ed., Robert Maynard Hutchins, vol. 49, *Great Books of the Western World* (Chicago: Encyclopaedia Britannica, Inc., 1952), 597.

[2] Carl Linnaeus, www.quotegarden.com/human.html (accessed December 11, 2006).

CHAPTER 2

[1] "Boy Uses $1.5 Million Painting for Gum Parker," Associated Press, March 1, 2006, www.msnbc.msn.com/id/11626023?GTI=7850 (accessed July 11, 2006).

[2] William Paley, *Natural Theology: or, Evidences of the Existence and Attributes of the Deity, Collected from the Appearances of Nature* (Hartford, CT: S. Andrus and Son, 1847), 1–2.

[3] www.creationscience.com/onlinebook/LifeSciences11.html.

[4] Charles Darwin, *The Origin of Species by Means of Natural Selection,* ed., Robert Maynard Hutchins, vol. 49, *Great Books of the Western World* (Chicago: Encyclopaedia Britannica, Inc., 1952), 85.

[5] "Sam: Beloved Ugly," CBS News, July 5, 2005, www/cbsnews.com/stories/2005/07/05/earlyshow/living/petplanet/main706245.shtml (accessed July 11, 2006).

[6] "Self-Injury No Longer Rare Among Teens," WebMD Medical News, www.webmd.com/content/article/53/61375.htm (accessed July 11, 2006).

[7] See the image at: www.art.com/asp/display_artist-asp/_/crid--32174/pg--10/Michelangelo_Buonarroti.htm (accessed January 8, 2007).

[8] Michelangelo, www.en.thinkexist.com/search/searchQuotation.asp?search=i+saw+the+angel+in+the+marble (accessed July 1, 2006).

CHAPTER 3

[1] Information in this section taken from www.wikipedia.org/wiki/1985_World_Series and www.wikipedia.org/wiki/Don_Denkinger.

CHAPTER 4

[1] "Text of President John Kennedy's Rice Stadium Moon Speech," www.vesuvius.jsc.nasa.gov/er/she/ricetalk.htm (accessed July 11, 2006).

[2] Neil Armstrong is often quoted as saying, "That's one small step for man," but according to many sources (including: www1.nasa.gov/audience/forstudents/5-8/features/F_Apollo_35th_Aniversary.html), he actually said, "That's one small step for a man . . ." (accessed August 14, 2006).

[3] "The Moon and Marilyn," *Apollo 13,* DVD, directed by Ron Howard (1998; Universal City, CA; Universal Home Video, Inc., 1998).

[4] Lao Tzu, www.en.thinkexist.com (accessed August 14, 2006).

CHAPTER 5

[1] Margot Morrell and Stephanie Capparell, *Shackleton's Way* (New York: Penguin Books, 2002), 1.

[2] Ibid., 40.

[3] Ibid., 54.

[4] Ibid., 56.

[5] Ibid., 63.

CHAPTER 6

[1] "Iraqi Man Ends 20 Years in Hiding," BBC News, www.news.bbc.co.uk/2/hi/middle_east/2938998.stm (accessed July 11, 2006).

CHAPTER 7

[1]James Strong, *The Strongest Strong's Exhaustive Concordance of the Bible* (Grand Rapids, MI: Zondervan, 2001), 1389.

CHAPTER 8

[1]As noted on: www.people.howstuffworks.com/question619.htm (accessed July 11, 2006).

[2]From the Frequently Asked Section page on: www.catholic.org/saints/faq.php (accessed July 11, 2006).

[3]William F. Arndt and F. Wilbur Gingrich, *A Greek-English Lexicon of the New Testament and Other Early Christian Literature* (Chicago: The University of Chicago Press, 1957, 1960), 10.

[4]Information in this section about Simeon the Stylite is from: www.saintpatrickdc.org/ss/0105.htm.

CHAPTER 9

[1]Information in this section from www.wikipedia.org/wiki/Jason_McElwain and www.usatoday.com/sports/preps/basketball/2006-02-23.

CHAPTER 10

[1]Robert Wiedersheim, *The Structure of Man: An Index to His Past History,* 2nd ed., trans. H. and M. Bernard (London: Macmillan and Co., 1895), 200.

[2]Information about Mike the Headless Chicken was taken from: www.miketheheadlesschicken.org/story.html. You can see his photo and join his fan club there too!

[3]These statistics are found on various sites, including www.sesamestreetpresents.org/PDFS/BodyFactsFinal.pdf and www.sci.monash.edu.au/msc/ptr/lessons/docs/biology/level4/muscular.ppt.

[4]www.wikipedia.org/wiki/Human_biology.

CHAPTER 11

[1]www.money.howstuffworks.com/question237.htm (accessed August 14, 2006).

[2]For an interesting study on the word *abba,* see Jack Cottrell, *Romans Volume 1* of *The College Press NIV Commentary* (Joplin, MO: College Press, 1996), 481–482.

[3]John Trent, "The Power of Words," *Men of Action,* Winter, 1993, p. 5, quoted in "Affirmation," *Sermon Illustrations* on www.bible.org/issus.asp?topic_id=34.

CHAPTER 13

[1]Information in this section taken from: www.pittsburghlive.com/x/pittsburghtrib/living/movies/oscars/s_340404.html and www.jamesjbraddock.com.

[2]"Man Tries to Convert Lions to Jesus, Gets Bitten," Reuters, MSNBC.com, November 3, 2004, www.msnbc.msn.com/id/6396422 (accessed August 14, 2006).

[3]Richard Carl Hoefler, *Will Daylight Come?* (Lima, Ohio: CSS Publishing Company, 1979), 25–27. Quoted by Steven Cole on www.net.bible.org/Illustration.php?topic_=689. Used by permission from CSS Publishing Company, 517 S. Main Street, Lima, Ohio 45804.

[4]www.imbd.com/title/tt0352248/quotes (accessed November 15, 2006).

ONE MORE THING TO REMEMBER

[1]Hans Christian Andersen, *Fairy Tales* (London: The Hamlyn Publishing Group Limited, 1959, 1974), 82.

For more information about the author
and his speaking and writing ministry,
visit the following:

www.arronchambers.com

www.christianstandard.com/MyLordandMyBlog

Other books by Arron Chambers:

Running on Empty: Life Lessons to Refuel Your Faith

*Scripture to Live By: True Stories and Spiritual Lessons
Inspired by the Word of God*

Also available . . .

- Second Guessing God
  978-0-7847-1841-4

- Second Guessing God (discussion guide)
  0-7847-1958-6

- Free Refill
  978-0-7847-1912-1

- Free Refill (discussion guide)
  978-0-7847-1992-3

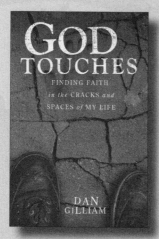

- God Touches
  978-0-7847-1963-3

- Soul Craving
  978-0-7847-1955-8

- Soul Craving (discussion guide)
  978-0-7847-1993-0